The Ultimate

UK Air Fryer Cookbook

Easy and Delicious Air Fryer Recipes for Beginners to Master the Art of Air Fryer Cooking

Pamela W. Newton

All Rights Reserved.

The contents of this book may not be reproduced, copied or transmitted without the direct written permission of the author or publisher. Under no circumstances will the publisher or the author be held responsible or liable for any damage, compensation or pecuniary loss arising directly or indirectly from the information contained in this book.

Legal notice. This book is protected by copyright. It is intended for personal use only. You may not modify, distribute, sell, use, quote or paraphrase any part or content of this book without the consent of the author or publisher.

Notice Of Disclaimer.

Please note that the information in this document is intended for educational and entertainment purposes only. Every effort has been made to provide accurate, up-to-date, reliable and complete information. No warranty of any kind is declared or implied. The reader acknowledges that the author does not engage in the provision of legal, financial, medical or professional advice. The content in this book has been obtained from a variety of sources. Please consult a licensed professional before attempting any of the techniques described in this book. By reading this document, the reader agrees that in no event shall the author be liable for any direct or indirect damages, including but not limited to errors, omissions or inaccuracies, resulting from the use of the information in this document.

CONTENTS

BREAD AND BREAKFAST

Blueberry Applesauce Oat Cake 11

All-in-one Breakfast Toast 11

Roasted Tomato And Cheddar Rolls . 11

Pesto Egg & Ham Sandwiches 12

Seasoned Herbed Sourdough Croutons 12

Colorful French Toast Sticks 13

White Wheat Walnut Bread 13

Banana-blackberry Muffins 13

Almond-pumpkin Porridge 14

Flank Steak With Caramelized Onions 14

Garlic Parmesan Bread Ring 15

Veggie & Feta Scramble Bowls 15

Zucchini Walnut Bread 16

Wake-up Veggie & Ham Bake 16

Vodka Basil Muffins With Strawberries 16

English Scones 17

Mushroom & Cavolo Nero Egg Muffins 17

Spinach-bacon Rollups 18

Lemon-blueberry Morning Bread 18

Seafood Quinoa Frittata 18

Blueberry Pannenkoek (dutch Pancake) 19

APPETIZERS AND SNACKS

Buffalo Wings 19

Cheeseburger Slider Pockets 20

Hot Cheese Bites 20

Chili Corn On The Cob 21

Eggplant Fries....................................21

Asian-style Shrimp Toast 22

Cheddar Stuffed Jalapenos.............22

Fiery Bacon-wrapped Dates 22

Enchilada Chicken Dip 23

Roasted Red Pepper Dip..................23

Crispy Spiced Chickpeas 24

Mustard Greens Chips With Curried Sauce 24

Bacon Candy....................................24

Cauliflower "tater" Tots...................25

Spicy Chicken And Pepper Jack Cheese Bites...25

Avocado Egg Rolls...........................26

Artichoke-spinach Dip 26

Beer Battered Onion Rings 27

Savory Eggplant Fries 27

Sweet Plantain Chips 28

Chipotle Sunflower Seeds 28

POULTRY RECIPES

Lemon Herb Whole Cornish Hen......29

Jerk Turkey Meatballs......................29

Gruyère Asparagus & Chicken Quiche 30

Nashville Hot Chicken......................30

Goat Cheese Stuffed Turkey Roulade 31

Yogurt-marinated Chicken Legs........31

Glazed Chicken Thighs....................32

Coconut Curry Chicken With Coconut Rice..32

Poblano Bake...................................33

Chicken & Fruit Biryani....................33

Berry-glazed Turkey Breast..............33

Turkey Scotch Eggs 34

Turkey Burgers.................................34

Chicken Chunks 35

Cal-mex Turkey Patties 35

Chicken Pigs In Blankets 35

Sweet Nutty Chicken Breasts 36

Windsor's Chicken Salad 36

Daadi Chicken Salad 37

Mexican Chicken Roll-ups 37

Popcorn Chicken Tenders With Vegetables 37

BEEF, PORK & LAMB RECIPES

Sloppy Joes 38

Crispy Steak Subs 38

Classic Salisbury Steak Burgers 39

Pork Schnitzel With Dill Sauce 39

Albóndigas 40

Skirt Steak With Horseradish Cream 41

Flank Steak With Roasted Peppers And Chimichurri 41

Perfect Pork Chops 42

Grilled Pork & Bell Pepper Salad 42

Pork Cutlets With Almond-lemon Crust 42

Ground Beef Calzones 43

Beef Short Ribs 43

Pork Schnitzel 44

Wiener Schnitzel 44

Lamb Meatballs With Quick Tomato Sauce 45

Barbecue-style London Broil 45

Suwon Pork Meatballs 46

Meatloaf With Tangy Tomato Glaze . 46

Crunchy Veal Cutlets 47

Calf's Liver 47

Italian Stuffed Bell Peppers 48

FISH AND SEAFOOD RECIPES

Feta & Shrimp Pita 49

Spiced Salmon Croquettes 49

Crispy Fish Sandwiches 49

Crab Stuffed Salmon Roast 50

Parmesan Fish Bites 50

Honey Pecan Shrimp 51

Sweet Potato–wrapped Shrimp 51

Chinese Fish Noodle Bowls 52

Lemon-dill Salmon Burgers 52

Almond-crusted Fish 53

Garlic And Dill Salmon 53

Cajun-seasoned Shrimp 54

Shrimp Teriyaki 54

Almond Topped Trout 54

Old Bay Lobster Tails 55

Yummy Salmon Burgers With Salsa Rosa 55

Southern Shrimp With Cocktail Sauce .. 56

Corn & Shrimp Boil 56

Lemon-roasted Salmon Fillets 56

Mediterranean Sea Scallops 57

Tilapia Teriyaki 57

VEGETARIAN RECIPES

Lentil Fritters 58

Pinto Bean Casserole 58

Lentil Burritos With Cilantro Chutney 59

Zucchini Tamale Pie 59

Eggplant Parmesan 60

Chili Tofu & Quinoa Bowls 60

Rigatoni With Roasted Onions, Fennel, Spinach And Lemon Pepper Ricotta . 61

Mushroom-rice Stuffed Bell Peppers 61

Sushi-style Deviled Eggs 62

Effortless Mac `n´ Cheese 62

Mushroom Lasagna 62

Spicy Sesame Tempeh Slaw With Peanut Dressing 63

Chive Potato Pierogi 64

Cheddar-bean Flautas 64

Easy Zucchini Lasagna Roll-ups 64

Vegetarian Stuffed Bell Peppers 65

Mexican Twice Air-fried Sweet Potatoes 65

Mushroom, Zucchini And Black Bean Burgers 66

Powerful Jackfruit Fritters 66

Italian-style Fried Cauliflower 67

Party Giant Nachos 67

VEGETABLE SIDE DISHES RECIPES

Garlic-parmesan Popcorn 68

Healthy Caprese Salad 68

Asparagus 68

Thyme Sweet Potato Wedges 69

Cauliflower 69

Crispy, Cheesy Leeks 69

Blistered Green Beans 70

Cheesy Texas Toast 70

Fried Green Tomatoes With Sriracha Mayo 70

Perfect Broccoli 71

Dijon Artichoke Hearts 71

Fried Cauliflower With Parmesan Lemon Dressing 72

Crispy Cauliflower Puffs 72

Panko-crusted Zucchini Fries 72

Salmon Salad With Steamboat Dressing 73

Roasted Ratatouille Vegetables 73

Roasted Herbed Shiitake Mushrooms 74

Baked Shishito Peppers 74

Glazed Carrots 74

Sweet Potato Curly Fries 75

Brown Rice And Goat Cheese Croquettes 75

SANDWICHES AND BURGERS RECIPES

Philly Cheesesteak Sandwiches 76

Inside Out Cheeseburgers 76

Lamb Burgers 77

Dijon Thyme Burgers 77

Thanksgiving Turkey Sandwiches 78

Chili Cheese Dogs 79

Black Bean Veggie Burgers 79

Salmon Burgers 80

Asian Glazed Meatballs 80

Mexican Cheeseburgers 81

White Bean Veggie Burgers 82

Inside-out Cheeseburgers 82

Chicken Gyros 83

Chicken Spiedies 83

Perfect Burgers 84

Thai-style Pork Sliders 84

Chicken Apple Brie Melt 85

Provolone Stuffed Meatballs 85

Sausage And Pepper Heros 86

Crunchy Falafel Balls 86

Eggplant Parmesan Subs 87

DESSERTS AND SWEETS

Sultana & Walnut Stuffed Apples 88

Banana-lemon Bars 88

Air-fried Strawberry Hand Tarts 88

Dark Chocolate Cream Galette 89

Brown Sugar Baked Apples 90

Air-fried Beignets 90

Carrot-oat Cake Muffins 90

Fried Oreos 91

Banana Bread Cake 91

Vanilla Cupcakes With Chocolate Chips 92

Homemade Chips Ahoy 92

Orange Gooey Butter Cake 93

Fried Oreos Recipes 93

Apple-carrot Cupcakes 94

Mini Carrot Cakes 94

Chocolate Cake 95

Berry Streusel Cake 95

Baked Caramelized Peaches 95

Sweet Potato Donut Holes 96

Annie's Chocolate Chunk Hazelnut Cookies 96

Lemon Iced Donut Balls 97

Recipes Index 98

INTRODUCTION

The Ultimate UK Air Fryer Cookbook: Easy and Delicious Air Fryer Recipes for Beginners to Master the Art of Air Fryer Cooking

Are you looking for a real BritIsh cookbook? If so, click the "Buy now" Button!
It is no secret that most of the Air Fryer Cookbooks on the marketplace are just a mere copy and paste of american style recipes, you just have to read a couple of reviews to realise it.

But the same can't be said about my book though!

Flavourful Recipes for Every Occasion
Discover a treasure trove of recipes designed to delight your taste buds and impress your guests. Whether you're hosting a dinner party or preparing a quick weeknight meal, find inspiration in our diverse collection of dishes. From hearty mains to tantalizing sides and decadent desserts, there's something for every palate and preference.

Easy-to-Follow Instructions for Foolproof Results
Save time and effort in the kitchen with our straightforward instructions and insider tips. Whether you're a seasoned chef or a novice cook, our recipes are designed for success every time. With step-by-step guidance, unlock the full potential of your air fryer and elevate your cooking skills to new heights.

Elevate Your Culinary Creations with Confidence
Expand your culinary repertoire and impress your loved ones with restaurant-quality dishes made right in your own kitchen. With the UK Air Fryer Cookbook as your guide, unleash your creativity and transform ordinary ingredients into extraordinary meals. From crispy appetizers to mouthwatering mains and decadent desserts, let your imagination soar.

This cookbook features a diverse range of recipes to satisfy every craving, including:

Energizing breakfasts to kickstart your day
Wholesome and fulfilling lunch recipes
Appetizers and snacks perfect for sharing and parties
Exquisite dinner options for memorable evenings
A range of poultry and meat dishes to satisfy all tastes
Seafood creations that taste like seaside holidays
Complementary side dishes to enhance every meal
Indulgent desserts for a sweet finish to your day
And lots more…

This book might be EXACTLY what you were looking for. Scroll Up and Click the "Buy Now" Button!

Bread And Breakfast

Blueberry Applesauce Oat Cake

Servings: 4 | Prep Time: 10 Minutes | Cooking Time: 65 Minutes

Ingredients:

- 1 cup applesauce
- 2/3 cup quick-cooking oats
- ½ tsp baking powder
- A pinch of salt
- ½ cup almond milk
- 5 tbsp almond flour
- 1 tbsp honey
- 1 egg
- 1 tsp vanilla extract
- ½ cup blueberries
- 4 tbsp grape preserves

Directions:

1. In a bowl, combine oats, baking powder, and salt.
2. In a larger bowl, combine milk, almond flour, honey, egg, and vanilla with a whisk until well mixed.
3. Add applesauce and stir until combined, then add the oat mixture.
4. Gently fold in blueberries.
5. Pour mixture into a greased baking dish. Spoon preserves over the top, but do not stir in.
6. Preheat air fryer to 149°C/300°F.
7. Place baking dish in air fryer and bake 25 minutes until golden and set.
8. Remove and allow to cool 10-15 minutes before slicing into 4 pieces. Serve warm.

Variations & Ingredients Tips:

- Use frozen or fresh berries.
- Substitute maple syrup for the honey.
- Top with a crumble topping before baking.

Per Serving: Calories: 220; Total Fat: 5g; Saturated Fat: 0.5g; Cholesterol: 35mg; Sodium: 85mg; Total Carbs: 40g; Dietary Fiber: 4g; Total Sugars: 20g; Protein: 5g

All-in-one Breakfast Toast

Servings: 1 | Prep Time: 5 Minutes | Cooking Time: 10 Minutes

Ingredients:

- 1 strip bacon, diced
- 1 slice 2.5cm thick bread
- 1 tablespoon softened butter (optional)
- 1 egg
- Salt and freshly ground black pepper
- ¼ cup grated Colby or Jack cheese

Directions:

1. Preheat air fryer to 205°C/400°F.
2. Air fry the bacon for 3 minutes, shaking basket occasionally. Remove bacon to a plate.
3. Use a paring knife to cut a circle halfway through the bread slice, creating an indentation. Spread butter in indentation if desired.
4. Transfer bread to air fryer basket, indentation side up. Crack egg into indentation and season with salt and pepper.
5. Air fry at 193°C/380°F for 5 minutes. Sprinkle cheese and bacon around egg yolk.
6. Air fry 1-2 more minutes until cheese melts and egg is cooked to desired doneness. Serve immediately.

Variations & Ingredients Tips:

- Use different cheese varieties like cheddar or Swiss
- Add veggies like spinach, tomatoes or avocado
- Cook the bacon fully before adding to get it extra crispy

Per Serving: Calories: 430; Total Fat: 27g; Saturated Fat: 12g; Cholesterol: 240mg; Sodium: 630mg; Total Carbs: 27g; Dietary Fiber: 1g; Total Sugars: 4g; Protein: 20g

Roasted Tomato And Cheddar Rolls

Servings: 12 | Prep Time: 30 Minutes | Cooking

Time: 55 Minutes

Ingredients:

- 4 Roma tomatoes
- ½ clove garlic, minced
- 1 tbsp olive oil
- ¼ tsp dried thyme
- Salt and pepper to taste
- 4 cups all-purpose flour
- 1 tsp active dry yeast
- 2 tsp sugar
- 2 tsp salt
- 1 tbsp olive oil
- 1 cup grated Cheddar cheese, plus more for sprinkling at the end
- 1½ cups water

Directions:

1. Toss tomatoes with garlic, 1 tbsp olive oil, thyme, salt and pepper.
2. Preheat air fryer to 200°C/390°F.
3. Air fry tomatoes cut-side up for 10 mins, shake, then 5-10 more mins at 165°C/330°F until no longer juicy. Cool and chop.
4. Mix flour, yeast, sugar, salt. Add 1 tbsp oil, tomatoes, cheese and knead with 1¼ cups water for 10 mins, adding more water as needed.
5. Let dough rise 1-2 hours. Divide into 12, roll into balls. Let rest 45 mins.
6. Preheat to 180°C/360°F. Spray dough balls and basket with oil.
7. Air fry 3 rolls at a time for 10 mins, adding cheese on top the last 2 mins.

Variations & Ingredients Tips:

- Add dried herbs, garlic or onions to the dough.
- Brush with egg wash before baking for a glossy finish.
- Fill with cheese, pesto or other fillings before rolling.

Per Serving: Calories: 274; Total Fat: 8g; Saturated Fat: 3g; Cholesterol: 14mg; Sodium: 501mg; Total Carbs: 42g; Dietary Fiber: 2g; Total Sugars: 2g; Protein: 8g

Pesto Egg & Ham Sandwiches

Servings: 2 | Prep Time: 10 Minutes | Cooking Time: 20 Minutes

Ingredients:

- 4 sandwich bread slices
- 2 tbsp butter, melted
- 4 eggs, scrambled
- 4 deli ham slices
- 2 Colby cheese slices
- 4 tsp basil pesto sauce
- ¼ tsp red chili flakes
- ¼ avocado, sliced

Directions:

1. Preheat air fryer at 190°C/370°F.
2. Brush 2 pieces of bread with half of the butter and place them, butter side down, into the frying basket. Divide eggs, chili flakes, sliced avocado, ham, and cheese on each bread slice.
3. Spread pesto on the remaining bread slices and place them, pesto side-down, onto the sandwiches. Brush the remaining butter on the tops of the sandwiches and Bake for 6 minutes, flipping once. Serve immediately.

Variations & Ingredients Tips:

- Use different cheese like cheddar or Swiss.
- Add sliced tomatoes or sauteed mushrooms.
- Substitute pesto with sundried tomato spread or olive tapenade.

Per Serving: Calories: 599; Total Fat: 39g; Saturated Fat: 16g; Cholesterol: 436mg; Sodium: 1176mg; Total Carbohydrates: 32g; Dietary Fiber: 4g; Total Sugars: 3g; Protein: 29g

Seasoned Herbed Sourdough Croutons

Servings: 4 | Prep Time: 5 Minutes | Cooking Time: 7 Minutes

Ingredients:

- 4 cups cubed sourdough bread, 2.5cm cubes (about 225-g)
- 1 tablespoon olive oil
- 1 teaspoon fresh thyme leaves
- ¼ – ½ teaspoon salt
- Freshly ground black pepper

Directions:

1. Combine all ingredients in a bowl and season to taste.
2. Preheat air fryer to 205°C/400°F.
3. Toss bread cubes into air fryer and cook for 7 minutes, shaking basket 1-2 times.

4. Serve warm or store in airtight container.

Variations & Ingredients Tips:

▶ Use different herb combinations like rosemary, sage or Italian seasoning.
▶ Add parmesan cheese or garlic powder for extra flavor.
▶ Toss croutons with a balsamic vinaigrette after cooking.

Per Serving: Calories: 117; Total Fat: 4g; Saturated Fat: 1g; Cholesterol: 0mg; Sodium: 310mg; Total Carbs: 18g; Dietary Fiber: 1g; Total Sugars: 1g; Protein: 3g

Colorful French Toast Sticks

Servings: 4 | Prep Time: 10 Minutes | Cooking Time: 20 Minutes

Ingredients:

- 1 egg
- ⅓ cup whole milk
- Salt to taste
- ½ teaspoon ground cinnamon
- ½ teaspoon ground chia seeds
- 1 cup crushed pebbles
- 4 sandwich bread slices, each cut into 4 sticks
- ¼ cup honey

Directions:

1. Preheat air fryer at 190°C/375°F.
2. Whisk the egg, milk, salt, cinnamon and chia seeds in a bowl. In another bowl, add crushed cereal.
3. Dip breadsticks in the egg mixture, then dredge them in the cereal crumbs.
4. Place breadsticks in the greased frying basket and Air Fry for 5 minutes, flipping once.
5. Serve with honey as a dip.

Variations & Ingredients Tips:

▶ Use different types of bread, such as whole wheat or brioche, for a variety of flavors and textures.
▶ Add some vanilla extract or orange zest to the egg mixture for extra flavor.
▶ For a savory version, replace the cinnamon and honey with garlic powder and marinara sauce for dipping.

Per Serving: Calories: 240; Total Fat: 5g; Saturated Fat: 1.5g; Cholesterol: 50mg; Sodium: 330mg; Total Carbs: 43g; Fiber: 2g; Sugars: 18g; Protein: 7g

White Wheat Walnut Bread

Servings: 8 | Prep Time: 5 Minutes | Cooking Time: 25 Minutes

Ingredients:

- 1 cup lukewarm water(40-46°C)
- 1 packet RapidRise yeast
- 1 tablespoon light brown sugar
- 2 cups whole-grain white wheat flour
- 1 egg, room temperature, beaten with a fork
- 2 teaspoons olive oil
- ½ teaspoon salt
- ½ cup chopped walnuts
- cooking spray

Directions:

1. In a small bowl, mix the water, yeast, and brown sugar.
2. Pour yeast mixture over flour and mix until smooth.
3. Add the egg, olive oil, and salt and beat with a wooden spoon for 2 minutes.
4. Stir in chopped walnuts. You will have very thick batter rather than stiff bread dough.
5. Spray air fryer baking pan with cooking spray and pour in batter, smoothing the top.
6. Let batter rise for 15 minutes.
7. Preheat air fryer to 180°C/360°F.
8. Cook bread for 25 minutes, until toothpick pushed into center comes out with crumbs clinging. Let bread rest for 10 minutes before removing from pan.

Variations & Ingredients Tips:

▶ Use different nuts like pecans or almonds instead of walnuts.
▶ Add dried fruits like cranberries or raisins to the batter.
▶ Brush the top with an egg wash before baking for a shiny crust.

Per Serving: Calories: 210; Total Fat: 8g; Saturated Fat: 1g; Cholesterol: 25mg; Sodium: 150mg; Total Carbs: 29g; Fiber: 4g; Sugars: 3g; Protein: 7g

Banana-blackberry Muffins

Servings: 6 | Prep Time: 10 Minutes | Cooking Time: 20 Minutes

Ingredients:

- 1 ripe banana, mashed
- ½ cup milk
- 1 tsp apple cider vinegar
- 1 tsp vanilla extract
- 2 tbsp ground flaxseed
- 2 tbsp coconut sugar
- ¾ cup all-purpose flour
- 1 tsp baking powder
- ½ tsp baking soda
- ¾ cup blackberries

Directions:

1. Preheat air fryer to 177°C/350°F.
2. Place banana in a bowl and stir in milk, vinegar, vanilla, flaxseed and coconut sugar.
3. In another bowl, combine flour, baking powder and baking soda.
4. Pour dry ingredients into banana mixture and stir gently to combine.
5. Divide batter between 6 muffin molds and top each with blackberries, pressing slightly.
6. Bake 16 minutes until golden brown and a toothpick comes out clean.
7. Allow to cool before serving.

Variations & Ingredients Tips:

- Use raspberries or blueberries instead of blackberries.
- Add chopped nuts or crystallized ginger to the batter.
- Substitute oat or almond milk for regular milk.

Per Serving: Calories: 125; Total Fat: 2g; Saturated Fat: 0g; Cholesterol: 0mg; Sodium: 170mg; Total Carbs: 25g; Dietary Fiber: 3g; Total Sugars: 9g; Protein: 3g

Almond-pumpkin Porridge

Servings: 4 | Prep Time: 10 Minutes | Cooking Time: 10 Minutes

Ingredients:

- 1 cup pumpkin seeds
- 2/3 cup chopped pecans
- 1/3 cup quick-cooking oats
- ¼ cup pumpkin purée
- ¼ cup diced pitted dates
- 1 tsp chia seeds
- 1 tsp sesame seeds
- 1 tsp dried berries
- 2 tbsp butter
- 2 tsp pumpkin pie spice
- ¼ cup honey
- 1 tbsp dark brown sugar
- ¼ cup almond flour
- Salt to taste

Directions:

1. Preheat air fryer at 177°C/350°F. Combine the pumpkin seeds, pecans, oats, pumpkin purée, dates, chia seeds, sesame seeds, dried berries, butter, pumpkin pie spice, honey, sugar, almond flour, and salt in a bowl. Press mixture into a greased cake pan. Place cake pan in the air fryer basket and bake for 5 minutes, stirring once. Let cool completely for 10 minutes before crumbling.

Variations & Ingredients Tips:

- Use different nuts like walnuts or almonds instead of pecans
- Substitute maple syrup for the honey
- Add cinnamon, nutmeg or cloves for extra spice

Per Serving: Calories: 490; Total Fat: 36g; Saturated Fat: 6g; Sodium: 85mg; Total Carbs: 37g; Dietary Fiber: 7g; Total Sugars: 22g; Protein: 10g

Flank Steak With Caramelized Onions

Servings: 2 | Prep Time: 10 Minutes | Cooking Time: 30 Minutes

Ingredients:

- 227 g flank steak, cubed
- 1 tablespoon mustard powder
- ½ teaspoon garlic powder
- 2 eggs
- 1 onion, sliced thinly
- Salt and pepper to taste

Directions:

1. Preheat air fryer to 180°C/360°F. Coat the flank steak cubes with mustard and garlic powders. Place them in the frying basket along with the onion and Bake for 3 minutes. Flip the steak over and gently stir the onions and cook for another 3 minutes. Push the steak and onions over to one side of the basket, creating space for heat-safe baking dish. Crack the eggs into a ceramic dish. Place the dish in the fryer. Cook for 15 minutes

at 160°C/320°F until the egg white are set and the onion is caramelized. Season with salt and pepper. Serve warm.

Variations & Ingredients Tips:

- Use sirloin, ribeye or tenderloin instead of flank steak.
- Add some sliced bell peppers or mushrooms to the onions.
- Top with crumbled blue cheese or goat cheese for a creamy element.

Per Serving: Calories: 426; Total Fat: 25g; Saturated Fat: 9g; Cholesterol: 328mg; Sodium: 263mg; Total Carbs: 10g; Dietary Fiber: 1g; Total Sugars: 4g; Protein: 41g

Garlic Parmesan Bread Ring

Servings: 6 | Prep Time: 15 Minutes | Cooking Time: 30 Minutes

Ingredients:

- ½ cup unsalted butter, melted
- ¼ teaspoon salt (omit if using salted butter)
- ¾ cup grated Parmesan cheese
- 3 to 4 cloves garlic, minced
- 1 tablespoon chopped fresh parsley
- 454 g frozen bread dough, defrosted
- olive oil
- 1 egg, beaten

Directions:

1. Combine the melted butter, salt, Parmesan cheese, garlic and chopped parsley in a small bowl.
2. Roll the dough out into a rectangle that measures 20 cm by 43 cm. Spread the butter mixture over the dough, leaving a 1.3 cm border un-buttered along one of the long edges. Roll the dough from one long edge to the other, ending with the un-buttered border. Pinch the seam shut tightly. Shape the log into a circle sealing the ends together by pushing one end into the other and stretching the dough around it.
3. Cut out a circle of aluminum foil that is the same size as the air fryer basket. Brush the foil circle with oil and place an oven safe ramekin or glass in the center. Transfer the dough ring to the aluminum foil circle, around the ramekin. This will help you make sure the dough will fit in the basket and maintain its ring shape. Use kitchen shears to cut 8 slits around the outer edge of the dough ring halfway to the center. Brush the dough ring with egg wash.
4. Preheat the air fryer to 200°C/400°F for 4 minutes. When it has Preheated, brush the sides of the basket with oil and transfer the dough ring, foil circle and ramekin into the basket. Slide the drawer back into the air fryer, but do not turn the air fryer on. Let the dough rise inside the warm air fryer for 30 minutes.
5. After the bread has proofed in the air fryer for 30 minutes, set the temperature to 170°C/340°F and air-fry the bread ring for 15 minutes. Flip the bread over by inverting it onto a plate or cutting board and sliding it back into the air fryer basket. Air-fry for another 15 minutes. Let the bread cool for a few minutes before slicing the bread ring in between the slits and serving warm.

Variations & Ingredients Tips:

- Add some dried herbs like basil, oregano or rosemary to the butter mixture.
- Sprinkle the top with everything bagel seasoning before baking for extra crunch and flavor.
- Serve with marinara sauce or ranch dressing for dipping.

Per Serving: Calories: 459; Total Fat: 27g; Saturated Fat: 15g; Cholesterol: 99mg; Sodium: 596mg; Total Carbs: 42g; Dietary Fiber: 2g; Total Sugars: 2g; Protein: 13g

Veggie & Feta Scramble Bowls

Servings: 2 | Prep Time: 10 Minutes | Cooking Time: 25 Minutes

Ingredients:

- 1 russet potato, cubed
- 1 bell pepper, cut into strips
- ½ feta, cubed
- 1 tbsp nutritional yeast
- ½ tsp garlic powder
- ½ tsp onion powder
- ¼ tsp ground turmeric
- 1 tbsp apple cider vinegar

Directions:

1. Preheat air fryer to 200°C/400°F.
2. Put in potato cubes and bell pepper strips and Air Fry for 10 minutes.
3. Combine the feta, nutritional yeast, garlic, onion, turmeric, and apple vinegar in a small pan.
4. Fit a trivet in the fryer, lay the pan on top, and Air Fry

for 5 more minutes until potatoes are tender and feta cheese cooked.
5. Share potatoes and bell peppers into 2 bowls and top with feta scramble. Serve.

Variations & Ingredients Tips:

- Add spinach, tomatoes or other veggies to the potato mix.
- Use firm or soft tofu instead of feta for a vegan option.
- Season with cumin, chili powder or other spices.

Per Serving: Calories: 282; Total Fat: 13g; Saturated Fat: 8g; Cholesterol: 50mg; Sodium: 666mg; Total Carbs: 28g; Dietary Fiber: 4g; Total Sugars: 3g; Protein: 14g

Zucchini Walnut Bread

Servings: 6 | Prep Time: 15 Minutes | Cooking Time: 30 Minutes

Ingredients:

- ¾ cup all-purpose flour
- ½ teaspoon baking soda
- 1 teaspoon ground cinnamon
- ⅛ teaspoon salt
- 1 large egg
- ⅓ cup packed brown sugar
- ¼ cup canola oil
- 1 teaspoon vanilla extract
- ⅓ cup milk
- 1 medium zucchini, shredded (about 1⅓ cups)
- ⅓ cup chopped walnuts

Directions:

1. Preheat the air fryer to 160°C/320°F.
2. In a medium bowl, mix together the flour, baking soda, cinnamon, and salt.
3. In a large bowl, whisk together the egg, brown sugar, oil, vanilla, and milk. Stir in the zucchini.
4. Slowly fold the dry ingredients into the wet ingredients. Stir in the chopped walnuts. Then pour the batter into two 10-cm oven-safe loaf pans.
5. Bake for 30 minutes or until a toothpick inserted into the center comes out clean. Let cool before slicing.
6. NOTE: Store tightly wrapped on the counter for up to 5 days, in the refrigerator for up to 10 days, or in the freezer for 3 months.

Variations & Ingredients Tips:

- Use whole wheat flour for a healthier twist.
- Add some raisins or dried cranberries for extra sweetness and texture.
- Sprinkle the top with cinnamon sugar before baking for a crunchy crust.

Per Serving: Calories: 260; Total Fat: 14g; Saturated Fat: 1g; Cholesterol: 30mg; Sodium: 180mg; Total Carbohydrates: 31g; Dietary Fiber: 1g; Total Sugars: 17g; Protein: 4g

Wake-up Veggie & Ham Bake

Servings: 4 | Prep Time: 10 Minutes | Cooking Time: 25 Minutes

Ingredients:

- 25 Brussels sprouts, halved
- 2 mini sweet peppers, diced
- 1 yellow onion, diced
- 3 deli ham slices, diced
- 2 tbsp orange juice
- ¼ tsp salt
- 1 tsp orange zest

Directions:

1. Preheat air fryer to 175°C/350°F.
2. Mix the sprouts, sweet peppers, onion, deli ham, orange juice, and salt in a bowl.
3. Transfer to the frying basket and Air Fry for 12 minutes, tossing once.
4. Scatter with orange zest and serve.

Variations & Ingredients Tips:

- Use turkey or chicken sausage instead of ham.
- Add diced sweet potatoes or butternut squash.
- Toss in maple syrup or balsamic vinegar before serving.

Per Serving: Calories: 100; Total Fat: 2g; Saturated Fat: 1g; Cholesterol: 15mg; Sodium: 480mg; Total Carbs: 15g; Dietary Fiber: 4g; Total Sugars: 6g; Protein: 7g

Vodka Basil Muffins With Strawberries

Servings: 6 | Prep Time: 10 Minutes | Cooking Time: 20 Minutes

Ingredients:

- ½ cup flour
- ½ cup granular sugar
- ½ tsp baking powder
- ⅛ tsp salt
- ½ cup chopped strawberries
- ¼ tsp vanilla extract
- 3 tbsp butter, melted
- 2 eggs
- ¼ tsp vodka
- 1 tbsp chopped basil

Directions:

1. Preheat air fryer to 190°C/375°F.
2. Combine the dry ingredients in a bowl. Set aside.
3. In another bowl, whisk the wet ingredients.
4. Pour wet ingredients into the bowl with the dry ingredients and gently combine.
5. Add basil and vodka to the batter. Do not overmix.
6. Spoon batter into six silicone cupcake liners lightly greased with olive oil.
7. Place liners in the frying basket and Bake for 7 minutes.
8. Let cool for 5 minutes onto a cooling rack before serving.

Variations & Ingredients Tips:

- Use other fresh herbs like thyme or rosemary instead of basil.
- Top with a lemon glaze or powdered sugar before serving.
- Add shredded zucchini or carrots to the batter for extra moisture.

Per Serving: Calories: 180; Total Fat: 8g; Saturated Fat: 4g; Cholesterol: 80mg; Sodium: 120mg; Total Carbs: 24g; Dietary Fiber: 1g; Total Sugars: 15g; Protein: 3g

English Scones

Servings: 8 | Prep Time: 15 Minutes | Cooking Time: 8 Minutes

Ingredients:

- 2 cups all-purpose flour
- 1 tablespoon baking powder
- ½ teaspoon salt
- 2 tablespoons sugar
- ¼ cup unsalted butter
- 158 ml plus 15 ml whole milk, divided

Directions:

1. Preheat the air fryer to 190°C/380°F.
2. In a large bowl, whisk together the flour, baking powder, salt, and sugar. Using a pastry blender or your fingers, cut in the butter until pea-size crumbles appear. Make a well in the center and pour in 158 ml of the milk. Quickly mix the batter until a ball forms. Knead the dough 3 times.
3. Place the dough onto a floured surface and, using your hands or a rolling pin, flatten the dough until it's 2 cm thick. Using a biscuit cutter or drinking glass, cut out 10 circles, reforming the dough and flattening as needed to use up the batter.
4. Brush the tops lightly with the remaining 15 ml of milk.
5. Place the scones into the air fryer basket. Cook for 8 minutes or until golden brown and cooked in the center.

Variations & Ingredients Tips:

- Add some dried currants, chocolate chips or chopped candied ginger to the dough.
- Sprinkle the tops with coarse sugar or brush with cream before baking.
- Serve with clotted cream, lemon curd or your favorite jam.

Per Serving: Calories: 218; Total Fat: 8g; Saturated Fat: 5g; Cholesterol: 21mg; Sodium: 292mg; Total Carbs: 32g; Dietary Fiber: 1g; Total Sugars: 4g; Protein: 5g

Mushroom & Cavolo Nero Egg Muffins

Servings: 6 | Prep Time: 10 Minutes | Cooking Time: 20 Minutes

Ingredients:

- 225g baby Bella mushrooms, sliced
- 6 eggs, beaten
- 1 garlic clove, minced
- Salt and pepper to taste
- 1/2 tsp chili powder
- 1 cup cavolo nero (Tuscan kale), shredded
- 2 scallions, diced

Directions:

1. Preheat air fryer to 160°C/320°F.
2. Place eggs, garlic, salt, pepper and chili powder in a

bowl and beat well combined.
3. Fold in mushrooms, cavolo nero and scallions.
4. Divide mixture between greased muffin cups and place in air fryer basket.
5. Bake for 12-15 minutes until eggs are set.
6. Cool 5 minutes before serving.

Variations & Ingredients Tips:

- Use different greens like spinach or chard.
- Add diced ham, bacon or cheese.
- Cook in oven-safe ramekins if air fryer cups are too small.

Per Serving: Calories: 75; Total Fat: 4g; Saturated Fat: 1g; Cholesterol: 155mg; Sodium: 90mg; Total Carbs: 4g; Dietary Fiber: 1g; Sugars: 2g; Protein: 6g

Spinach-bacon Rollups

Servings: 4 | Prep Time: 10 Minutes | Cooking Time: 9 Minutes

Ingredients:

- 4 flour tortillas (15-18cm size)
- 4 slices Swiss cheese
- 1 cup baby spinach leaves
- 4 slices turkey bacon

Directions:

1. Preheat air fryer to 200°C/390°F.
2. On each tortilla, place one slice cheese, ¼ cup spinach.
3. Roll up tortillas and wrap each with a bacon slice, securing ends with toothpicks.
4. Place rollups spaced apart in air fryer basket.
5. Cook 4 mins, turn and rearrange, cook 5 more mins until bacon is crisp.

Variations & Ingredients Tips:

- Use different cheese varieties like cheddar or pepper jack.
- Add diced tomatoes, olives or roasted red peppers.
- Brush with beaten egg before cooking for a crispier crust.

Per Serving: Calories: 252; Total Fat: 13g; Saturated Fat: 5g; Cholesterol: 36mg; Sodium: 677mg; Total Carbs: 20g; Dietary Fiber: 1g; Total Sugars: 1g; Protein: 13g

Lemon-blueberry Morning Bread

Servings: 2 | Prep Time: 5 Minutes | Cooking Time: 15 Minutes

Ingredients:

- 60 g flour
- 30 g powdered sugar
- ½ teaspoon baking powder
- ⅛ teaspoon salt
- 2 tablespoons butter, melted
- 1 egg
- ½ teaspoon gelatin
- ½ teaspoon vanilla extract
- 1 teaspoon lemon zest
- ½ cup blueberries

Directions:

1. Preheat air fryer to 150°C/300°F. Mix the flour, sugar, baking powder, and salt in a bowl. In another bowl, whisk the butter, egg, gelatin, lemon zest, vanilla extract, and blueberries. Add egg mixture to flour mixture and stir until smooth. Spoon mixture into a pizza pan. Place pan in the frying basket and Bake for 10 minutes. Let sit for 5 minutes before slicing. Serve immediately.

Variations & Ingredients Tips:

- Use raspberries, blackberries or chopped strawberries instead of blueberries.
- Add some poppy seeds or chopped nuts to the batter for texture.
- Top with a dollop of lemon curd or cream cheese frosting.

Per Serving: Calories: 320; Total Fat: 14g; Saturated Fat: 8g; Cholesterol: 123mg; Sodium: 298mg; Total Carbs: 44g; Dietary Fiber: 2g; Total Sugars: 23g; Protein: 6g

Seafood Quinoa Frittata

Servings: 4 | Prep Time: 10 Minutes | Cooking Time: 30 Minutes

Ingredients:

- ½ cup cooked shrimp, chopped
- ½ cup cooked quinoa
- ½ cup baby spinach
- 4 eggs
- ½ tsp dried basil

- 1 anchovy, chopped
- ½ cup grated cheddar

Directions:

1. Preheat air fryer to 160°C/320°F.
2. Add quinoa, shrimp, and spinach to a greased baking pan. Set aside.
3. Beat eggs, anchovy, and basil in a bowl until frothy.
4. Pour over the quinoa mixture, then top with cheddar cheese.
5. Bake until frittata is puffed and golden, 14-18 minutes.
6. Serve.

Variations & Ingredients Tips:

- Use other cooked proteins like chicken or salmon.
- Substitute different greens like kale or arugula.
- Top with sliced avocado, salsa or hot sauce.

Per Serving: Calories: 235; Total Fat: 10g; Saturated Fat: 5g; Cholesterol: 222mg; Sodium: 421mg; Total Carbs: 15g; Dietary Fiber: 2g; Total Sugars: 1g; Protein: 21g

Blueberry Pannenkoek (dutch Pancake)

Servings: 4 | Prep Time: 5 Minutes | Cooking Time: 30 Minutes

Ingredients:

- 3 eggs, beaten
- ½ cup buckwheat flour
- ½ cup milk
- ½ tsp vanilla
- 1 ½ cups blueberries, crushed
- 2 tbsp powdered sugar

Directions:

1. Preheat air fryer to 165°C/330°F.
2. Mix together eggs, buckwheat flour, milk, and vanilla in a bowl.
3. Pour the batter into a greased baking pan and add it to the fryer.
4. Bake until the pancake is puffed and golden, 12-16 minutes.
5. Remove pan and flip pancake over onto a plate.
6. Top with crushed blueberries and powdered sugar. Serve.

Variations & Ingredients Tips:

- Use a cast iron or oven-safe skillet instead of a baking pan.
- Add lemon zest or cinnamon to the batter.
- Top with maple syrup or fruit compote.

Per Serving: Calories: 170; Total Fat: 3g; Saturated Fat: 1g; Cholesterol: 110mg; Sodium: 45mg; Total Carbs: 30g; Dietary Fiber: 3g; Total Sugars: 9g; Protein: 6g

Appetizers And Snacks

Buffalo Wings

Servings: 2 | Prep Time: 10 Minutes (plus 2 Hours Marinating Time) | Cooking Time: 12 Minutes Per Batch

Ingredients:

- 900-g chicken wings
- 3 tablespoons butter, melted
- ¼ cup hot sauce
- Finishing Sauce:
- 3 tablespoons butter, melted
- ¼ cup hot sauce
- 1 teaspoon Worcestershire sauce

Directions: | Prepare the chicken wings by cutting off the wing tips and discarding (or freezing for chicken stock). Divide the drumettes from the wingettes by cutting through the joint. Place the chicken wing pieces in a large bowl.

7. Combine the melted butter and the hot sauce and stir to blend well. Pour the marinade over the chicken wings, cover and let the wings marinate for 2 hours or up to overnight in the refrigerator.
8. Preheat the air fryer to 200°C/400°F.
9. Air-fry the wings in two batches for 10 minutes per batch, shaking the basket halfway through the cooking process. When both batches are done, toss all the wings back into the basket for another 2 minutes to heat through and finish cooking.
10. While the wings are air-frying, combine the remaining 3 tbsp of butter, 60ml of hot sauce and the Worcestershire sauce. Remove the wings from the air fryer, toss them in the finishing sauce and serve with some cooling blue cheese dip and celery sticks.

Variations & Ingredients Tips:

- Adjust the amount of hot sauce to make the wings milder or spicier.
- Use a different hot sauce like sriracha or gochujang for an Asian twist.
- Sprinkle the wings with garlic powder, onion powder, or smoked paprika before air frying for extra flavor.

Per Serving: Calories: 620; Total Fat: 50g; Saturated Fat: 24g; Cholesterol: 220mg; Sodium: 1780mg; Total Carbohydrates: 2g; Dietary Fiber: 0g; Total Sugars: 0g; Protein: 41g

Cheeseburger Slider Pockets

Servings: 4 | Prep Time: 25 Minutes | Cooking Time: 13 Minutes

Ingredients:

- 450 g extra lean ground beef
- 2 teaspoons steak seasoning
- 2 tablespoons Worcestershire sauce
- 225 g Cheddar cheese
- ⅓ cup ketchup
- ¼ cup light mayonnaise
- 1 tablespoon pickle relish
- 450 g frozen bread dough, defrosted
- 1 egg, beaten
- sesame seeds
- vegetable or olive oil, in a spray bottle

Directions:

1. Combine the ground beef, steak seasoning and Worcestershire sauce in a large bowl. Divide the meat mixture into 12 equal portions. Cut the Cheddar cheese into twelve 5 cm squares, about 6 mm thick. Stuff a square of cheese into the center of each portion of meat and shape into an 8 cm patty.
2. Make the slider sauce by combining the ketchup, mayonnaise, and relish in a small bowl. Set aside.
3. Cut the bread dough into twelve pieces. Shape each piece of dough into a ball and use a rolling pin to roll them out into 10 cm circles. Dollop ½ teaspoon of the slider sauce into the center of each dough circle. Place a beef patty on top of the sauce and wrap the dough around the patty, pinching the dough together to seal the pocket shut. Try not to stretch the dough too much when bringing the edges together. Brush both sides of the slider pocket with the beaten egg. Sprinkle sesame seeds on top of each pocket.
4. Preheat the air fryer to 175°C/350°F.
5. Spray or brush the bottom of the air fryer basket with oil. Air-fry the slider pockets four at a time. Transfer the slider pockets to the air fryer basket, seam side down and air-fry at 175°C/350°F for 10 minutes, until the dough is golden brown. Flip the slider pockets over and air-fry for another 3 minutes. When all the batches are done, pop all the sliders into the air fryer for a few minutes to re-heat and serve them hot out of the fryer.

Variations & Ingredients Tips:

- Use ground turkey or chicken instead of beef for a leaner version.
- Add some sautéed mushrooms, onions or bacon to the cheese stuffing.
- Brush with garlic butter or sprinkle with everything bagel seasoning before cooking.

Per Serving: Calories: 782; Total Fat: 42g; Saturated Fat: 19g; Cholesterol: 183mg; Sodium: 1567mg; Total Carbs: 57g; Dietary Fiber: 3g; Total Sugars: 9g; Protein: 45g

Hot Cheese Bites

Servings: 6 | Prep Time: 15 Minutes | Cooking Time: 30 Minutes + Cooling Time

Ingredients:

- 1/3 cup grated Velveeta cheese
- 1/3 cup shredded American cheese
- 113 g cream cheese
- 2 jalapeños, finely chopped
- ½ cup bread crumbs

- 2 egg whites
- ½ cup all-purpose flour

Directions:

1. Preheat air fryer to 200°C/400°F. Blend the cream cheese, Velveeta, American cheese, and jalapeños in a bowl. Form the mixture into 2.5 cm balls. Arrange them on a sheet pan and freeze for 15 minutes.
2. Spread the flour, egg, and bread crumbs in 3 separate bowls. Once the cheese balls are removed from the freezer, dip them first in flour, then in the egg and finally in the crumbs. Air Fry for 8 minutes in the previously greased frying basket. Flip the balls and cook for another 4 minutes until crispy. Serve warm.

Variations & Ingredients Tips:

- Use pepper jack, cheddar or mozzarella cheese for different flavors.
- Add some chopped bacon, ham or chorizo to the cheese mixture.
- Serve with ranch dressing, marinara sauce or salsa for dipping.

Per Serving: Calories: 211; Total Fat: 13g; Saturated Fat: 7g; Cholesterol: 44mg; Sodium: 556mg; Total Carbs: 14g; Dietary Fiber: 1g; Total Sugars: 2g; Protein: 10g

Chili Corn On The Cob

Servings: 4 | Prep Time: 10 Minutes | Cooking Time: 30 Minutes

Ingredients:

- Salt and pepper to taste
- ½ tsp smoked paprika
- ¼ tsp chili powder
- 4 ears corn, halved
- 1 tbsp butter, melted
- ¼ cup lime juice
- 1 tsp lime zest
- 1 lime, quartered

Directions:

1. Preheat air fryer to 200°C/400°F. Combine salt, pepper, lime juice, lime zest, paprika, and chili powder in a small bowl. Toss corn and butter in a large bowl, then add the seasonings from the small bowl. Toss until coated. Arrange the corn in a single layer in the frying basket. Air Fry for 10 minutes, then turn the corn. Air Fry for another 8 minutes. Squeeze lime over the corn and serve.

Variations & Ingredients Tips:

- Brush the cooked corn with mayonnaise and sprinkle with cotija cheese for Mexican street corn.
- Use lemon juice and zest instead of lime for a different citrus flavor.
- Sprinkle with chopped fresh herbs like cilantro or parsley before serving.

Per Serving: Calories: 133; Total Fat: 5g; Saturated Fat: 2g; Cholesterol: 8mg; Sodium: 254mg; Total Carbs: 23g; Dietary Fiber: 3g; Total Sugars: 6g; Protein: 4g

Eggplant Fries

Servings: 18 | Prep Time: 15 Minutes | Cooking Time: 10 Minutes

Ingredients:

- ¾ cup All-purpose flour or tapioca flour
- 1 Large egg(s), well beaten
- 1 cup Seasoned Italian-style dried bread crumbs (gluten-free, if a concern)
- 3 tablespoons (about 15 g) Finely grated Asiago or Parmesan cheese
- 3 Peeled 13 mm thick eggplant slices (each about 7.5 cm in diameter)
- Olive oil spray

Directions:

1. Preheat the air fryer to 190°C/375°F (or 195°C/380°F or 200°C/390°F, if one of these is the closest setting).
2. Set up and fill three shallow soup plates or small pie plates on your counter: one for the flour, one for the egg(s), and one for the bread crumbs mixed with the cheese until well combined.
3. Cut each eggplant slice into six 13 mm wide strips or sticks. Dip one strip in the flour, coating it well on all sides. Gently shake off the excess flour, then dip the strip in the beaten egg(s) to coat it without losing the flour. Let any excess egg slip back into the rest, then roll the strip in the bread-crumb mixture to coat evenly on all sides, even the ends. Set the strips aside on a cutting board and continue dipping and coating the remaining strips as you did the first one.
4. Generously coat the strips with olive oil spray on all sides. Set them in the basket in one layer and air-fry undisturbed for 10 minutes, or until golden brown and crisp. If the machine is at 200°C/390°F, the strips may

be done in 8 minutes.
5. Remove the basket from the machine and cool for a couple of minutes. Then use kitchen tongs to transfer the eggplant fries to a wire rack to cool for only a minute or two more before serving.

Variations & Ingredients Tips:

- Use panko breadcrumbs for a crunchier coating.
- Add some garlic powder, onion powder or smoked paprika to the breading.
- Serve with marinara sauce, ranch dressing or tzatziki for dipping.

Per Serving: Calories: 50; Total Fat: 2g; Saturated Fat: 0g; Cholesterol: 12mg; Sodium: 108mg; Total Carbs: 7g; Dietary Fiber: 1g; Total Sugars: 1g; Protein: 2g

Asian-style Shrimp Toast

Servings: 4 | Prep Time: 15 Minutes | Cooking Time: 25 Minutes

Ingredients:

- 8 large raw shrimp, chopped
- 1 egg white
- 2 garlic cloves, minced
- 1 red chili, minced
- 1 celery stalk, minced
- 2 tbsp cornstarch
- ¼ tsp Chinese five-spice
- 3 firm bread slices

Directions:

1. Preheat air fryer to 175°C/350°F. Add the shrimp, egg white, garlic, red chili, celery, corn starch, and five-spice powder in a bowl and combine. Place 1/3 of the shrimp mix on a slice of bread, smearing it to the edges, then slice the bread into 4 strips. Lay the strips in the frying basket in a single layer and Air Fry for 3-6 minutes until golden and crispy. Repeat until all strips are cooked. Serve hot.

Variations & Ingredients Tips:

- Use crabmeat instead of shrimp for a different flavor.
- Add some grated ginger to the shrimp mixture.
- Serve with a sweet chili sauce for dipping.

Per Serving: Calories: 130; Total Fat: 2g; Saturated Fat: 0g; Cholesterol: 49mg; Sodium: 319mg; Total Carbs: 19g; Dietary Fiber: 1g; Total Sugars: 2g; Protein: 9g

Cheddar Stuffed Jalapenos

Servings: 5 | Prep Time: 10 Minutes | Cooking Time: 15 Minutes

Ingredients:

- 10 jalapeño peppers
- 170 g ricotta cheese
- ¼ cup grated cheddar
- 2 tbsp bread crumbs

Directions:

1. Preheat air fryer to 170°C/340°F. Cut jalapeños in half lengthwise. Clean out the seeds and membrane. Set aside. Microwave ricotta cheese in a small bowl for 15 seconds to soften. Stir in cheddar cheese to combine. Stuff each jalapeño half with the cheese mixture. Top the poppers with bread crumbs. Place in air fryer and lightly spray with cooking oil. Bake for 5-6 minutes. Serve warm.

Variations & Ingredients Tips:

- Add some cooked bacon bits or chorizo to the cheese filling.
- Top with a slice of pepper jack cheese before air frying.
- Serve with ranch or queso dip for dunking.

Per Serving: Calories: 156; Total Fat: 10g; Saturated Fat: 6g; Cholesterol: 38mg; Sodium: 204mg; Total Carbs: 7g; Dietary Fiber: 1g; Total Sugars: 2g; Protein: 10g

Fiery Bacon-wrapped Dates

Servings: 16 | Prep Time: 15 Minutes | Cooking Time: 6 Minutes

Ingredients:

- 8 Thin-cut bacon strips, halved widthwise (gluten-free, if a concern)
- 16 Medium or large Medjool dates, pitted
- 3 tablespoons (about 20 g) Shredded semi-firm mozzarella
- 32 Pickled jalapeño rings

Directions:

1. Preheat the air fryer to 200°C/400°F.
2. Lay a bacon strip half on a clean, dry work surface. Split one date lengthwise without cutting through it,

so that it opens like a pocket. Set it on one end of the bacon strip and open it a bit. Place 1 teaspoon of the shredded cheese and 2 pickled jalapeño rings in the date, then gently squeeze it together without fully closing it (just to hold the stuffing inside). Roll up the date in the bacon strip and set it bacon seam side down on a cutting board. Repeat this process with the remaining bacon strip halves, dates, cheese, and jalapeño rings.
3. Place the bacon-wrapped dates bacon seam side down in the basket. Air-fry undisturbed for 6 minutes, or until crisp and brown.
4. Use kitchen tongs to gently transfer the wrapped dates to a wire rack or serving platter. Cool for a few minutes before serving.

Variations & Ingredients Tips:

- Stuff the dates with blue cheese, goat cheese or cream cheese instead of mozzarella.
- Wrap the dates with prosciutto or pancetta instead of bacon.
- Drizzle with honey, balsamic glaze or hot honey before serving.

Per Serving: Calories: 57; Total Fat: 2g; Saturated Fat: 1g; Cholesterol: 6mg; Sodium: 117mg; Total Carbs: 9g; Dietary Fiber: 1g; Total Sugars: 8g; Protein: 2g

Enchilada Chicken Dip

Servings: 6 | Prep Time: 10 Minutes | Cooking Time: 20 Minutes

Ingredients:

- 1 cup chopped cooked chicken breasts
- 1 can diced green chiles, including juice
- 225 g cream cheese, softened
- ¼ cup mayonnaise
- ¼ cup sour cream
- 2 tbsp chopped onion
- 1 jalapeño pepper, minced
- 1 cup shredded mozzarella
- ¼ cup diced tomatoes
- 1 tsp chili powder

Directions:

1. Preheat air fryer to 200°C/400°F. Beat the cream cheese, mayonnaise, and sour cream in a bowl until smooth. Stir in the cooked chicken, onion, green chiles, jalapeño, and ½ cup of mozzarella cheese. Spoon the mixture into a baking dish. Sprinkle the remaining cheese on top, and place the dish in the fryer. Bake for 10 minutes. Garnish the dip with diced tomatoes and chili powder. Serve.

Variations & Ingredients Tips:

- Use leftover rotisserie chicken, turkey or pork instead of chicken breasts.
- Add some black beans, corn or diced bell peppers to the dip.
- Serve with tortilla chips, pita chips or veggie sticks for dipping.

Per Serving: Calories: 297; Total Fat: 23g; Saturated Fat: 11g; Cholesterol: 94mg; Sodium: 405mg; Total Carbs: 7g; Dietary Fiber: 1g; Total Sugars: 4g; Protein: 16g

Roasted Red Pepper Dip

Servings: 2 | Prep Time: 10 Minutes | Cooking Time: 15 Minutes

Ingredients:

- 2 medium-size red bell peppers
- 425 g canned white beans, drained and rinsed
- 1 tbsp fresh oregano leaves, packed
- 3 tbsp olive oil
- 1 tbsp lemon juice
- ½ tsp table salt
- ½ tsp ground black pepper

Directions:

1. Preheat the air fryer to 200°C/400°F. Set the peppers in the basket and air-fry undisturbed for 15 minutes, until blistered and even blackened. Use kitchen tongs to transfer the peppers to a zip-closed plastic bag or small bowl. Seal the bag or cover the bowl with plastic wrap. Set aside for 20 minutes. Peel each pepper, then stem it, cut it in half, and remove all its seeds and their white membranes. Set the pieces of the pepper in a food processor. Add the beans, oregano, olive oil, lemon juice, salt, and pepper. Cover and process until smooth, stopping the machine at least once to scrape down the inside of the canister. Scrape the dip into a bowl and serve warm, or cover and refrigerate for up to 3 days (although the dip tastes best if it's allowed to come back to room temperature).

Variations & Ingredients Tips:

- Roast a head of garlic along with the peppers and add the cloves to the dip for a deeper flavor.

- Use cannellini beans, chickpeas, or black beans instead of white beans for a different taste and texture.
- Add smoked paprika, cumin, or hot sauce for a smoky or spicy kick.

Per Serving: Calories: 437; Total Fat: 22g; Saturated Fat: 3g; Cholesterol: 0mg; Sodium: 886mg; Total Carbs: 47g; Dietary Fiber: 12g; Total Sugars: 3g; Protein: 17g

Crispy Spiced Chickpeas

Servings: 2 | Prep Time: 5 Minutes | Cooking Time: 20 Minutes

Ingredients:

- 1 (425 g) can chickpeas, drained (or 1½ cups cooked chickpeas)
- ½ teaspoon salt
- ½ teaspoon chili powder
- ¼ teaspoon ground cinnamon
- ⅛ teaspoon smoked paprika
- pinch ground cayenne pepper
- 1 tablespoon olive oil

Directions:

1. Preheat the air fryer to 200°C/400°F.
2. Dry the chickpeas as well as you can with a clean kitchen towel, rubbing off any loose skins as necessary. Combine the spices in a small bowl. Toss the chickpeas with the olive oil and then add the spices and toss again.
3. Air-fry for 15 minutes, shaking the basket a couple of times while they cook.
4. Check the chickpeas to see if they are crispy enough and if necessary, air-fry for another 5 minutes to crisp them further. Serve warm, or cool to room temperature and store in an airtight container for up to two weeks.

Variations & Ingredients Tips:

- Try different spice blends like curry powder, garam masala or taco seasoning.
- Add some grated Parmesan cheese or nutritional yeast after cooking.
- Serve as a topping for salads or soups, or as a healthy snack.

Per Serving: Calories: 224; Total Fat: 9g; Saturated Fat: 1g; Cholesterol: 0mg; Sodium: 716mg; Total Carbs: 29g; Dietary Fiber: 8g; Total Sugars: 5g; Protein: 9g

Mustard Greens Chips With Curried Sauce

Servings: 4 | Prep Time: 10 Minutes | Cooking Time: 20 Minutes

Ingredients:

- 1 cup plain yogurt
- 1 tbsp lemon juice
- 1 tbsp curry powder
- 1 bunch of mustard greens
- 2 tsp olive oil
- Sea salt to taste

Directions:

1. Preheat air fryer to 200°C/390°F. Using a sharp knife, remove and discard the ribs from the mustard greens. Slice the leaves into 5-8 cm pieces. Transfer them to a large bowl, then pour in olive oil and toss to coat. Air fry for 5-6 minutes, shaking at least once. The chips should be crispy when finished. Sprinkle with a little bit of sea salt. Mix the yogurt, lemon juice, salt, and curry in a small bowl. Serve the greens with the sauce.

Variations & Ingredients Tips:

- Try using kale, collard greens, or Swiss chard instead of mustard greens for different flavors.
- Add a pinch of cayenne pepper or paprika to the sauce for a spicy kick.
- Garnish with chopped fresh cilantro or mint for added freshness.

Per Serving: Calories: 92; Total Fat: 5g; Saturated Fat: 1g; Cholesterol: 5mg; Sodium: 149mg; Total Carbs: 8g; Dietary Fiber: 2g; Total Sugars: 4g; Protein: 5g

Bacon Candy

Servings: 6 | Prep Time: 5 Minutes | Cooking Time: 6 Minutes

Ingredients:

- 1½ tablespoons Honey
- 1 teaspoon White wine vinegar
- 3 Extra thick–cut bacon strips, halved widthwise (gluten-free, if a concern)
- ½ teaspoon Ground black pepper

Directions:

1. Preheat the air fryer to 175°C/350°F.
2. Whisk the honey and vinegar in a small bowl until incorporated.
3. When the machine is at temperature, remove the basket. Lay the bacon strip halves in the basket in one layer. Brush the tops with the honey mixture; sprinkle each bacon strip evenly with black pepper.
4. Return the basket to the machine and air-fry undisturbed for 6 minutes, or until the bacon is crunchy. Or a little less time if you prefer bacon that's still pliable, an extra minute if you want the bacon super crunchy. Take care that the honey coating doesn't burn. Remove the basket from the machine and set aside for 5 minutes. Use kitchen tongs to transfer the bacon strips to a serving plate.

Variations & Ingredients Tips:

- Sprinkle with some cayenne pepper for a spicy-sweet combo.
- Use maple syrup instead of honey for a different flavor.
- Dip the cooked bacon in melted chocolate and let harden for a decadent treat.

Per Serving: Calories: 63; Total Fat: 4g; Saturated Fat: 1g; Cholesterol: 10mg; Sodium: 181mg; Total Carbs: 4g; Dietary Fiber: 0g; Total Sugars: 4g; Protein: 3g

Cauliflower "tater" Tots

Servings: 6 | Prep Time: 20 Minutes | Cooking Time: 10 Minutes

Ingredients:

- 1 head of cauliflower
- 2 eggs
- ¼ cup all-purpose flour*
- ½ cup grated Parmesan cheese
- 1 teaspoon salt
- freshly ground black pepper
- vegetable or olive oil, in a spray bottle

Directions:

1. Grate the head of cauliflower with a box grater or finely chop it in a food processor. You should have about 3½ cups. Place the chopped cauliflower in the center of a clean kitchen towel and twist the towel tightly to squeeze all the water out of the cauliflower. (This can be done in two batches to make it easier to drain all the water from the cauliflower.)
2. Place the squeezed cauliflower in a large bowl. Add the eggs, flour, Parmesan cheese, salt and freshly ground black pepper. Shape the cauliflower into small cylinders or "tater tot" shapes, rolling roughly one tablespoon of the mixture at a time. Place the tots on a cookie sheet lined with paper towel to absorb any residual moisture. Spray the cauliflower tots all over with oil.
3. Preheat the air fryer to 200°C/400°F.
4. Air-fry the tots at 200°C/400°F, one layer at a time for 10 minutes, turning them over for the last few minutes of the cooking process for even browning. Season with salt and black pepper. Serve hot with your favorite dipping sauce.

Variations & Ingredients Tips:

- Add some shredded cheese, bacon bits or chopped herbs to the mixture.
- Make them into larger patties for cauliflower hash browns.
- Serve with ketchup, ranch dressing or sriracha mayo for dipping.

Per Serving: Calories: 113; Total Fat: 6g; Saturated Fat: 3g; Cholesterol: 63mg; Sodium: 548mg; Total Carbs: 8g; Dietary Fiber: 3g; Total Sugars: 3g; Protein: 7g

Spicy Chicken And Pepper Jack Cheese Bites

Servings: 8 | Prep Time: 20 Minutes + Chilling Time | Cooking Time: 8 Minutes

Ingredients:

- 225 g cream cheese, softened
- 2 cups grated pepper jack cheese
- 1 jalapeño pepper, diced
- 2 scallions, minced
- 1 tsp paprika
- 2 tsp salt, divided
- 3 cups shredded cooked chicken
- ¼ cup all-purpose flour*
- 2 eggs, lightly beaten
- 1 cup panko breadcrumbs*
- olive oil, in a spray bottle
- salsa

Directions:

1. Beat the cream cheese in a bowl until it is smooth and easy to stir. Add the pepper jack cheese, jalapeño pepper, scallions, paprika and 1 teaspoon of salt. Fold in

25

the shredded cooked chicken and combine well. Roll this mixture into 2.5-cm balls. Set up a dredging station with three shallow dishes. Place the flour into one shallow dish. Place the eggs into a second shallow dish. Finally, combine the panko breadcrumbs and remaining teaspoon of salt in a third dish. Coat the chicken cheese balls by rolling each ball in the flour first, then dip them into the eggs and finally roll them in the panko breadcrumbs to coat all sides. Refrigerate for at least 30 minutes. Preheat the air fryer to 200°C/400°F. Spray the chicken cheese balls with oil and air-fry in batches for 8 minutes. Shake the basket a few times throughout the cooking process to help the balls brown evenly. Serve hot with salsa on the side.

Variations & Ingredients Tips:

- Use a mixture of cheddar, mozzarella, and Parmesan cheese for a milder flavor.
- Add chopped bacon, ham, or chorizo for a meatier bite.
- Serve with ranch dressing, honey mustard, or BBQ sauce for dipping.

Per Serving: Calories: 341; Total Fat: 24g; Saturated Fat: 12g; Cholesterol: 143mg; Sodium: 892mg; Total Carbohydrates: 9g; Dietary Fiber: 1g; Total Sugars: 1g; Protein: 23g

Avocado Egg Rolls

Servings: 8 | Prep Time: 25 Minutes | Cooking Time: 8 Minutes

Ingredients:

- 8 full-size egg roll wrappers
- 1 medium avocado, sliced into 8 pieces
- 1 cup cooked black beans, divided
- ½ cup mild salsa, divided
- ½ cup shredded Mexican cheese, divided
- 80 ml filtered water, divided
- ½ cup sour cream
- 1 teaspoon chipotle hot sauce

Directions:

1. Preheat the air fryer to 200°C/400°F.
2. Place the egg roll wrapper on a flat surface and place 1 strip of avocado down in the center.
3. Top the avocado with 2 tablespoons of black beans, 1 tablespoon of salsa, and 1 tablespoon of shredded cheese.
4. Place two of your fingers into the water, and then moisten the four outside edges of the egg roll wrapper with water (so the outer edges will secure shut).
5. Fold the bottom corner up, covering the filling. Then secure the sides over the top, remembering to lightly moisten them so they stick. Tightly roll the egg roll up and moisten the final flap of the wrapper and firmly press it into the egg roll to secure it shut.
6. Repeat Steps 2–5 until all 8 egg rolls are complete.
7. When ready to cook, spray the air fryer basket with olive oil spray and place the egg rolls into the basket. Depending on the size and type of air fryer you have, you may need to do this in two sets.
8. Cook for 4 minutes, flip, and then cook the remaining 4 minutes.
9. Repeat until all the egg rolls are cooked. Meanwhile, mix the sour cream with the hot sauce to serve as a dipping sauce.
10. Serve warm.

Variations & Ingredients Tips:

- Add some cooked shredded chicken or pork to the filling.
- Use pepper jack cheese for extra spice.
- Serve with guacamole or queso dip.

Per Serving: Calories: 226; Total Fat: 11g; Saturated Fat: 4g; Cholesterol: 17mg; Sodium: 473mg; Total Carbs: 25g; Dietary Fiber: 4g; Total Sugars: 2g; Protein: 7g

Artichoke-spinach Dip

Servings: 4 | Prep Time: 10 Minutes | Cooking Time: 25 Minutes

Ingredients:

- 113 g canned artichoke hearts, chopped
- ½ cup Greek yogurt
- ¼ cup cream cheese
- ½ cup spinach, chopped
- ½ red bell pepper, chopped
- 1 garlic clove, minced
- ½ tsp dried oregano
- 3 tsp grated Parmesan cheese

Directions:

1. Preheat air fryer to 170°C/340°F. Mix the yogurt and cream cheese. Add the artichoke, spinach, red bell pepper, garlic, and oregano, then put the mix in a pan and scatter Parmesan cheese on top. Put the pan in the fry-

ing basket and Bake for 9-14 minutes. The dip should be bubbly and brown. Serve hot.

Variations & Ingredients Tips:

- Add some jalapeños or red pepper flakes for a spicy kick.
- Top with shredded mozzarella before cooking for extra cheesiness.
- Serve with sliced baguette, pita chips or fresh vegetables for dipping.

Per Serving: Calories: 126; Total Fat: 9g; Saturated Fat: 5g; Cholesterol: 19mg; Sodium: 288mg; Total Carbs: 7g; Dietary Fiber: 2g; Total Sugars: 3g; Protein: 6g

Beer Battered Onion Rings

Servings: 2 | Prep Time: 20 Minutes | Cooking Time: 16 Minutes

Ingredients:

- 80 g flour
- ½ teaspoon baking soda
- 1 teaspoon paprika
- 1 teaspoon salt
- ½ teaspoon freshly ground black pepper
- 180 ml beer
- 1 egg, beaten
- 1½ cups fine breadcrumbs
- 1 large Vidalia onion, peeled and sliced into 13 mm rings
- vegetable oil

Directions:

1. Set up a dredging station. Mix the flour, baking soda, paprika, salt and pepper together in a bowl. Pour in the beer, add the egg and whisk until smooth. Place the breadcrumbs in a cake pan or shallow dish.
2. Separate the onion slices into individual rings. Dip each onion ring into the batter with a fork. Lift the onion ring out of the batter and let any excess batter drip off. Then place the onion ring in the breadcrumbs and shake the cake pan back and forth to coat the battered onion ring. Pat the ring gently with your hands to make sure the breadcrumbs stick and that both sides of the ring are covered. Place the coated onion ring on a sheet pan and repeat with the rest of the onion rings.
3. Preheat the air fryer to 180°C/360°F.
4. Lightly spray the onion rings with oil, coating both sides. Layer the onion rings in the air fryer basket, stacking them on top of each other in a haphazard manner.
5. Air-fry for 10 minutes at 180°C/360°F. Flip the onion rings over and rotate the onion rings from the bottom of the basket to the top. Air-fry for an additional 6 minutes.
6. Serve immediately with your favorite dipping sauce.

Variations & Ingredients Tips:

- Use sparkling water instead of beer for a non-alcoholic version.
- Add some cayenne pepper or hot sauce to the batter for a spicy kick.
- Serve with ranch dressing, chipotle mayo or marinara sauce for dipping.

Per Serving: Calories: 456; Total Fat: 12g; Saturated Fat: 2g; Cholesterol: 93mg; Sodium: 1733mg; Total Carbs: 71g; Dietary Fiber: 5g; Total Sugars: 8g; Protein: 14g

Savory Eggplant Fries

Servings: 4 | Prep Time: 10 Minutes | Cooking Time: 20 Minutes

Ingredients:

- 1 eggplant, sliced
- 2 1/2 tbsp soy sauce
- 2 tsp garlic powder
- 2 tsp onion powder
- 4 tsp olive oil
- 2 tbsp fresh basil, chopped

Directions:

1. Preheat air fryer to 390°F/200°C. Place the eggplant slices in a bowl and sprinkle the soy sauce, garlic, onion, and oil on top. Coat the eggplant evenly. Place the eggplant in a single layer in the greased frying basket and Air Fry for 5 minutes. Remove and put the eggplant in the bowl again. Toss the eggplant slices to coat evenly with the remaining liquid and put back in the fryer. Roast for another 3 minutes. Remove the basket and flip the pieces over to ensure even cooking. Roast for another 5 minutes or until the eggplant is golden. Top with basil and serve.

Variations & Ingredients Tips:

- Use breadcrumbs or panko for extra crunch.
- Add grated parmesan on top after cooking.
- Serve with marinara sauce for dipping.

Per Serving: Calories: 101; Total Fat: 7g; Saturated Fat: 1g; Cholesterol: 0mg; Sodium: 670mg; Total Carbs: 9g; Dietary Fiber: 3g; Total Sugars: 4g; Protein: 2g

Sweet Plantain Chips

Servings: 4 | Prep Time: 10 Minutes | Cooking Time: 11 Minutes

Ingredients:

- 2 very ripe plantains, peeled and sliced into 2.5-cm pieces
- Vegetable oil spray
- 3 tbsp maple syrup
- For garnishing coarse sea salt or kosher salt

Directions:

1. Pour about 120 ml water into the bottom of your air fryer basket or into a metal tray on a lower rack in some models. Preheat the air fryer to 200°C/400°F. Put the plantain pieces in a bowl, coat them with vegetable oil spray, and toss gently, spraying at least one more time and tossing repeatedly, until the pieces are well coated. When the machine is at temperature, arrange the plantain pieces in the basket in one layer. Air-fry undisturbed for 5 minutes. Remove the basket from the machine and spray the back of a metal spatula with vegetable oil spray. Use the spatula to press down on the plantain pieces, spraying it again as needed, to flatten the pieces to about half their original height. Brush the plantain pieces with maple syrup, then return the basket to the machine and continue air-frying undisturbed for 6 minutes, or until the plantain pieces are soft and caramelized. Use kitchen tongs to transfer the pieces to a serving platter. Sprinkle the pieces with salt and cool for a couple of minutes before serving. Or cool to room temperature before serving, about 1 hour.

Variations & Ingredients Tips:

▶ Sprinkle the chips with cinnamon sugar, chili powder, or grated Parmesan cheese for different flavors.
▶ Serve with guacamole, salsa, or black bean dip for a savory twist.
▶ For a healthier version, use less maple syrup or substitute honey or agave nectar.

Per Serving: Calories: 193; Total Fat: 1g; Saturated Fat: 0g; Sodium: 147mg; Total Carbohydrates: 48g; Dietary Fiber: 3g; Total Sugars: 28g; Protein: 1g

Chipotle Sunflower Seeds

Servings: 4 | Prep Time: 5 Minutes | Cooking Time: 20 Minutes

Ingredients:

- 2 cups sunflower seeds
- 2 tsp olive oil
- ½ tsp chipotle powder
- 1 garlic clove, minced
- ¼ tsp salt
- 1 tsp granulated sugar

Directions:

1. Preheat air fryer to 165°C/325°F. In a bowl, mix the sunflower seeds, olive oil, chipotle powder, garlic, salt, and sugar until well coated. Place the mixture in the frying basket and Air Fry for 10 minutes, shaking once. Serve chilled.

Variations & Ingredients Tips:

▶ Use pumpkin seeds or cashews instead of sunflower seeds.
▶ Add some smoked paprika or cumin for extra smoky flavor.
▶ Toss the seeds with some lime juice and chopped cilantro after cooking.

Per Serving: Calories: 374; Total Fat: 33g; Saturated Fat: 4g; Cholesterol: 0mg; Sodium: 154mg; Total Carbs: 12g; Dietary Fiber: 5g; Total Sugars: 3g; Protein: 12g

Poultry Recipes

Lemon Herb Whole Cornish Hen

Servings: 2 | Prep Time: 15 Minutes | Cooking Time: 50 Minutes

Ingredients:

- 1 Cornish hen
- 1/4 cup olive oil
- 2 tbsp lemon juice
- 2 tbsp sage, chopped
- 2 tbsp thyme, chopped
- 4 garlic cloves, chopped
- Salt and pepper to taste
- 1 celery stalk, chopped
- 1/2 small onion
- 1/2 lemon, juiced and zested
- 2 tbsp chopped parsley

Directions:

1. Preheat air fryer to 190°C/380°F.
2. Whisk the olive oil, lemon juice, sage, thyme, garlic, salt, and pepper in a bowl. Rub the mixture on the tops and sides of the hen. Pour any excess inside the cavity of the bird.
3. Stuff the celery, onion, and lemon juice and zest into the cavity of the hen.
4. Put in the frying basket and Roast for 40-45 minutes.
5. Cut the hen in half and serve garnished with parsley.

Variations & Ingredients Tips:

▶ Use orange juice and zest for a different citrus flavor.
▶ Add sliced garlic and butter under the skin before cooking.
▶ Serve with roasted potatoes and a green salad.

Per Serving: Calories: 720; Total Fat: 55g; Saturated Fat: 13g; Cholesterol: 255mg; Sodium: 340mg; Total Carbs: 7g; Dietary Fiber: 2g; Total Sugars: 2g; Protein: 51g

Jerk Turkey Meatballs

Servings: 7 | Prep Time: 15 Minutes | Cooking Time: 8 Minutes

Ingredients:

- 450g lean ground turkey
- 1/4 cup chopped onion
- 1 teaspoon minced garlic
- 1/2 teaspoon dried thyme
- 1/4 teaspoon ground cinnamon
- 1 teaspoon cayenne pepper
- 1/2 teaspoon paprika
- 1/2 teaspoon salt
- 1/8 teaspoon black pepper
- 1/4 teaspoon red pepper flakes
- 2 teaspoons brown sugar
- 1 large egg, whisked
- 1/3 cup panko breadcrumbs
- 2 1/3 cups cooked brown Jasmine rice
- 2 green onions, chopped
- 3/4 cup sweet onion dressing

Directions:

1. Preheat the air fryer to 175°C/350°F.
2. In a medium bowl, mix the ground turkey with the onion, garlic, thyme, cinnamon, cayenne pepper, paprika, salt, pepper, red pepper flakes, and brown sugar. Add the whisked egg and stir in the breadcrumbs until the turkey starts to hold together.
3. Using a 30-ml scoop, portion the turkey into meatballs. You should get about 28 meatballs.
4. Spray the air fryer basket with olive oil spray.
5. Place the meatballs into the air fryer basket and cook for 5 minutes, shake the basket, and cook another 2 to 4 minutes (or until the internal temperature of the meatballs reaches 74°C/165°F).
6. Remove the meatballs from the basket and repeat for the remaining meatballs.
7. Serve warm over a bed of rice with chopped green onions and spicy Caribbean jerk dressing.

Variations & Ingredients Tips:

▶ Use ground chicken or pork instead of turkey.
▶ Add diced bell peppers or carrots to the meatball mix.

▶ Serve in lettuce wraps or slider buns.

Per Serving: Calories: 300; Total Fat: 11g; Saturated Fat: 2.5g; Cholesterol: 85mg; Sodium: 450mg; Total Carbs: 28g; Dietary Fiber: 2g; Total Sugars: 5g; Protein: 22g

Gruyère Asparagus & Chicken Quiche

Servings: 4 | Prep Time: 15 Minutes | Cooking Time: 30 Minutes

Ingredients:

- 1 grilled chicken breast, diced
- 1/2 cup (55g) shredded Gruyère cheese
- 1 premade pie crust
- 2 eggs, beaten
- 1/4 cup milk
- Salt and pepper to taste
- 225g asparagus, sliced
- 1 lemon, zested

Directions:

1. Preheat air fryer to 180°C/360°F.
2. Carefully press the crust into a baking dish, trimming the edges. Prick the dough with a fork a few times.
3. Add the eggs, milk, asparagus, salt, pepper, chicken, lemon zest, and half of Gruyère cheese to a mixing bowl and stir until completely blended. Pour the mixture into the pie crust.
4. Bake in the air fryer for 15 minutes. Sprinkle the remaining Gruyère cheese on top of the quiche filling. Bake for 5 more minutes until the quiche is golden brown.
5. Remove and allow to cool for a few minutes before cutting. Serve sliced and enjoy!

Variations & Ingredients Tips:

▶ Use Swiss or cheddar cheese instead of Gruyère.
▶ Add sautéed mushrooms or spinach to the filling.
▶ Make a crustless quiche for a low-carb option.

Per Serving: Calories: 330; Total Fat: 22g; Saturated Fat: 10g; Cholesterol: 150mg; Sodium: 420mg; Total Carbs: 16g; Dietary Fiber: 1g; Total Sugars: 2g; Protein: 18g

Nashville Hot Chicken

Servings: 4 | Prep Time: 20 Minutes | Cooking Time: 27 Minutes

Ingredients:

- 1 (1.8kg) chicken, cut into 6 pieces (2 breasts, 2 thighs and 2 drumsticks)
- 2 eggs
- 1 cup buttermilk
- 2 cups all-purpose flour
- 2 tablespoons paprika
- 1 teaspoon garlic powder
- 1 teaspoon onion powder
- 2 teaspoons salt
- 1 teaspoon freshly ground black pepper
- Vegetable oil, in a spray bottle
- Nashville Hot Sauce:
- 1 tablespoon cayenne pepper
- 1 teaspoon salt
- 1/4 cup vegetable oil
- 4 slices white bread
- Dill pickle slices

Directions:

1. Cut the chicken breasts into 2 pieces so that you have a total of 8 pieces of chicken.
2. Set up a two-stage dredging station. Whisk the eggs and buttermilk together in a bowl. Combine the flour, paprika, garlic powder, onion powder, salt and black pepper in a zipper-sealable plastic bag. Dip the chicken pieces into the egg-buttermilk mixture, then toss them in the seasoned flour, coating all sides. Repeat this procedure (egg mixture and then flour mixture) one more time. This can be a little messy, but make sure all sides of the chicken are completely covered. Spray the chicken with vegetable oil and set aside.
3. Preheat the air fryer to 190°C/370°F. Spray or brush the bottom of the air-fryer basket with a little vegetable oil.
4. Air-fry the chicken in two batches at 190°C/370°F for 20 minutes, flipping the pieces over halfway through the cooking process. Transfer the chicken to a plate, but do not cover. Repeat with the second batch of chicken.
5. Lower the temperature on the air fryer to 170°C/340°F. Flip the chicken back over and place the first batch of chicken on top of the second batch already in the basket. Air-fry for another 7 minutes.
6. While the chicken is air-frying, combine the cayenne pepper and salt in a bowl. Heat the vegetable oil in a small saucepan and when it is very hot, add it to the spice mix, whisking until smooth. It will sizzle briefly

when you add it to the spices.

7. Place the fried chicken on top of the white bread slices and brush the hot sauce all over chicken. Top with the pickle slices and serve warm. Enjoy the heat and the flavor!

Variations & Ingredients Tips:

- Adjust the cayenne to your spice preference.
- Use chicken tenders for easier prep and cooking.
- Serve in a sandwich with coleslaw and comeback sauce.

Per Serving: Calories: 860; Total Fat: 58g; Saturated Fat: 12g; Cholesterol: 290mg; Sodium: 2210mg; Total Carbs: 36g; Dietary Fiber: 2g; Total Sugars: 5g; Protein: 55g

Goat Cheese Stuffed Turkey Roulade

Servings: 4 | Prep Time: 20 Minutes | Cooking Time: 55 Minutes

Ingredients:

- 1 boneless turkey breast, skinless
- Salt and pepper to taste
- 115g goat cheese
- 1 tbsp marjoram
- 1 tbsp sage
- 2 garlic cloves, minced
- 2 tbsp olive oil
- 2 tbsp chopped cilantro

Directions:

1. Preheat air fryer to 190°C/380°F.
2. Butterfly the turkey breast with a sharp knife and season with salt and pepper.
3. Mix together the goat cheese, marjoram, sage, and garlic in a bowl. Spread the cheese mixture over the turkey breast, then roll it up tightly, tucking the ends underneath.
4. Put the turkey breast roulade onto a piece of aluminum foil, wrap it up, and place it into the air fryer. Bake for 30 minutes.
5. Turn the turkey breast, brush the top with oil, and then continue to cook for another 10-15 minutes.
6. Slice and serve sprinkled with cilantro.

Variations & Ingredients Tips:

- Use feta or ricotta cheese instead of goat cheese.
- Add some chopped sun-dried tomatoes or spinach to the filling.
- Drizzle with balsamic glaze before serving.

Per Serving: Calories: 330; Total Fat: 16g; Saturated Fat: 6g; Cholesterol: 125mg; Sodium: 340mg; Total Carbs: 1g; Dietary Fiber: 0g; Total Sugars: 0g; Protein: 45g

Yogurt-marinated Chicken Legs

Servings: 4 | Prep Time: 10 Minutes (plus Marinating Time) | Cooking Time: 50 Minutes

Ingredients:

- 1 cup Greek yogurt
- 1 tbsp Dijon mustard
- 1 tsp smoked paprika
- 1 tbsp crushed red pepper
- 1 tsp garlic powder
- 1 tsp dried oregano
- 1 tsp dried thyme
- 1 teaspoon ground cumin
- 1/4 cup lemon juice
- Salt and pepper to taste
- 680g chicken legs
- 3 tbsp butter, melted

Directions:

1. Combine all ingredients, except chicken and butter, in a bowl. Fold in chicken legs and toss until coated. Let sit covered in the fridge for 60 minutes up to overnight.
2. Preheat air fryer at 190°C/375°F. Shake excess marinade from chicken; place them in the greased frying basket and Air Fry for 18 minutes, brush melted butter and flip once.
3. Let chill for 5 minutes before serving.

Variations & Ingredients Tips:

- Use buttermilk or coconut milk instead of yogurt for a different flavor profile.
- Add grated ginger or turmeric to the marinade for an Indian twist.
- Serve with mint-cucumber raita or mango chutney on the side.

Per Serving: Calories: 470; Total Fat: 30g; Saturated Fat: 12g; Cholesterol: 245mg; Sodium: 510mg; Total Carbs: 5g; Dietary Fiber: 1g; Total Sugars: 3g; Protein: 45g

Glazed Chicken Thighs

Servings: 4 | Prep Time: 10 Minutes | Cooking Time: 25 Minutes

Ingredients:

- 450g boneless, skinless chicken thighs
- 1/4 cup balsamic vinegar
- 3 tbsp honey
- 2 tbsp brown sugar
- 1 tsp whole-grain mustard
- 1/4 cup soy sauce
- 3 garlic cloves, minced
- Salt and pepper to taste
- 1/2 tsp smoked paprika
- 2 tbsp chopped shallots

Directions:

1. Preheat air fryer to 190°C/375°F.
2. Whisk vinegar, honey, sugar, soy sauce, mustard, garlic, salt, pepper, and paprika in a small bowl.
3. Arrange the chicken in the frying basket and brush the top of each with some of the vinegar mixture. Air Fry for 7 minutes, then flip the chicken. Brush the tops with the rest of the vinegar mixture and Air Fry for another 5 to 8 minutes.
4. Allow resting for 5 minutes before slicing. Serve warm sprinkled with shallots.

Variations & Ingredients Tips:

- Use maple syrup instead of honey for a different sweetness.
- Add some red pepper flakes to the glaze for heat.
- Serve over rice or salad greens.

Per Serving: Calories: 320; Total Fat: 8g; Saturated Fat: 2g; Cholesterol: 140mg; Sodium: 960mg; Total Carbs: 31g; Dietary Fiber: 0g; Total Sugars: 27g; Protein: 32g

Coconut Curry Chicken With Coconut Rice

Servings: 4 | Prep Time: 20 Minutes (plus Marinating Time) | Cooking Time: 56 Minutes

Ingredients:

- 1 (400-ml) can coconut milk
- 2 tablespoons green or red curry paste
- Zest and juice of one lime
- 1 clove garlic, minced
- 1 tablespoon grated fresh ginger
- 1 teaspoon ground cumin
- 1 (1.4 to 1.8-kg) chicken, cut into 8 pieces
- Vegetable or olive oil
- Salt and freshly ground black pepper
- Fresh cilantro leaves
- For the rice:
- 1 cup basmati or jasmine rice
- 1 cup water
- 1 cup coconut milk
- 1/2 teaspoon salt
- Freshly ground black pepper

Directions:

1. Make the marinade by combining the coconut milk, curry paste, lime zest and juice, garlic, ginger and cumin. Coat the chicken on all sides with the marinade and marinate the chicken for 1 hour to overnight in the refrigerator.
2. Preheat the air fryer to 190°C/380°F.
3. Brush the bottom of the air fryer basket with oil. Transfer the chicken thighs and drumsticks from the marinade to the air fryer basket, letting most of the marinade drip off. Season to taste with salt and freshly ground black pepper.
4. Air-fry the chicken drumsticks and thighs at 190°C/380°F for 12 minutes. Flip the chicken over and continue to air-fry for another 12 minutes. Set aside and air-fry the chicken breast pieces at 190°C/380°F for 15 minutes. Turn the chicken breast pieces over and air-fry for another 12 minutes. Return the chicken thighs and drumsticks to the air fryer and air-fry for an additional 5 minutes.
5. While the chicken is cooking, make the coconut rice. Rinse the rice kernels with water and drain well. Place the rice in a medium saucepan with a tight fitting lid, along with the water, coconut milk, salt and freshly ground black pepper. Bring the mixture to a boil and then cover, reduce the heat and let it cook gently for 20 minutes without lifting the lid. When the time is up, lift the lid, fluff with a fork and set aside.
6. Remove the chicken from the air fryer and serve warm with the coconut rice and fresh cilantro scattered around.

Variations & Ingredients Tips:

- Adjust the amount of curry paste to your spice preference.
- Use boneless, skinless chicken thighs for a quicker cooking time.

- Garnish with chopped peanuts or cashews for extra crunch.

Per Serving: Calories: 670; Total Fat: 42g; Saturated Fat: 29g; Cholesterol: 150mg; Sodium: 580mg; Total Carbs: 34g; Dietary Fiber: 1g; Total Sugars: 1g; Protein: 40g

Poblano Bake

Servings: 4 | Prep Time: 15 Minutes | Cooking Time: 11 Minutes Per Batch

Ingredients:

- 2 large poblano peppers (approx. 14 cm long excluding stem)
- 340g ground turkey, raw
- 3/4 cup cooked brown rice
- 1 teaspoon chile powder
- 1/2 teaspoon ground cumin
- 1/2 teaspoon garlic powder
- 115g sharp Cheddar cheese, grated
- 1 (225g) jar salsa, warmed

Directions:

1. Slice each pepper in half lengthwise so that you have four wide, flat pepper halves.
2. Remove seeds and membrane and discard. Rinse inside and out.
3. In a large bowl, combine turkey, rice, chile powder, cumin, and garlic powder. Mix well.
4. Divide turkey filling into 4 portions and stuff one into each of the 4 pepper halves. Press lightly to pack down.
5. Place 2 pepper halves in air fryer basket and cook at 200°C/390°F for 10 minutes or until turkey is well done.
6. Top each pepper half with 1/4 of the grated cheese. Cook 1 more minute or just until cheese melts.
7. Repeat steps 5 and 6 to cook remaining pepper halves.
8. To serve, place each pepper half on a plate and top with 60 ml/1/4 cup warm salsa.

Variations & Ingredients Tips:

- Use ground beef or chicken instead of turkey.
- Add some cooked black beans or corn to the filling.
- Top with sliced avocado, sour cream or chopped cilantro.

Per Serving: Calories: 340; Total Fat: 19g; Saturated Fat: 8g; Cholesterol: 105mg; Sodium: 660mg; Total Carbs: 15g; Dietary Fiber: 2g; Total Sugars: 3g; Protein: 29g

Chicken & Fruit Biryani

Servings: 4 | Prep Time: 10 Minutes | Cooking Time: 30 Minutes

Ingredients:

- 3 chicken breasts, cubed
- 2 tsp olive oil
- 2 tbsp cornstarch
- 1 tbsp curry powder
- 1 apple, chopped
- ½ cup chicken broth
- 1/3 cup dried cranberries
- 1 cup cooked basmati rice

Directions:

1. Preheat air fryer to 190°C/380°F.
2. Combine the chicken and olive oil, then add some cornstarch and curry powder. Mix to coat, then add the apple and pour the mix in a baking pan.
3. Put the pan in the air fryer and Bake for 8 minutes, stirring once.
4. Add the chicken broth, cranberries, and 2 tbsp of water and continue baking for 10 minutes, letting the sauce thicken. The chicken should be lightly charred and cooked through.
5. Serve warm with basmati rice.

Variations & Ingredients Tips:

- Substitute chicken with cauliflower florets or paneer cheese for a vegetarian version.
- Use raisins, apricots, or figs instead of cranberries.
- Add a pinch of saffron or cardamom to the rice for extra aroma.

Per Serving: Calories: 350; Total Fat: 7g; Saturated Fat: 1g; Sodium: 250mg; Total Carbohydrates: 43g; Dietary Fiber: 4g; Total Sugars: 17g; Protein: 30g

Berry-glazed Turkey Breast

Servings: 4 | Prep Time: 15 Minutes | Cooking Time: 1 Hour 25 Minutes

Ingredients:

- 1 bone-in, skin-on turkey breast
- 1 tbsp olive oil
- Salt and pepper to taste
- 1 cup raspberries

- 1 cup chopped strawberries
- 2 tbsp balsamic vinegar
- 2 tbsp butter, melted
- 1 tbsp honey mustard
- 1 tsp dried rosemary

Directions:

1. Preheat the air fryer to 180°C/350°F.
2. Lay the turkey breast skin-side up in the air fryer basket, brush with the oil, and sprinkle with salt and pepper.
3. Bake for 55-65 minutes, flipping twice.
4. Meanwhile, mix the berries, vinegar, melted butter, rosemary and honey mustard in a blender and blend until smooth.
5. Turn the turkey skin-side up inside the fryer and brush with half of the berry mix. Bake for 5 more minutes.
6. Put the remaining berry mix in a small saucepan and simmer for 3-4 minutes while the turkey cooks.
7. When the turkey is done, let it stand for 10 minutes, then carve. Serve with the remaining glaze.

Variations & Ingredients Tips:

- Use boneless, skinless turkey breast for quicker cooking time.
- Substitute raspberries and strawberries with blackberries, blueberries, or cranberries.
- Add a pinch of cayenne pepper or red pepper flakes to the glaze for a spicy kick.

Per Serving: Calories: 400; Total Fat: 15g; Saturated Fat: 5g; Sodium: 180mg; Total Carbohydrates: 14g; Dietary Fiber: 3g; Total Sugars: 10g; Protein: 52g

Turkey Scotch Eggs

Servings: 4 | Prep Time: 20 Minutes | Cooking Time: 30 Minutes

Ingredients:

- 680g ground turkey
- 1 tbsp ground cumin
- 1 tsp ground coriander
- 2 garlic cloves, minced
- 3 raw eggs
- 1 1/2 cups bread crumbs
- 6 hard-cooked eggs, peeled
- 1/2 cup flour

Directions:

1. Preheat air fryer to 190°C/370°F.
2. Place the ground turkey, cumin, coriander, garlic, one egg, and 1/2 cup of bread crumbs in a large bowl and mix until well incorporated.
3. Divide into 6 equal portions, then flatten each into long ovals. Set aside.
4. In a shallow bowl, beat the remaining raw eggs. In another shallow bowl, add flour. Do the same with another plate for bread crumbs.
5. Roll each cooked egg in flour, then wrap with one oval of chicken sausage until completely covered.
6. Roll again in flour, then coat in the beaten egg before rolling in bread crumbs.
7. Arrange the eggs in the greased frying basket. Air Fry for 12-14 minutes, flipping once until the sausage is cooked and the eggs are brown.
8. Serve.

Variations & Ingredients Tips:

- Use ground pork or beef instead of turkey.
- Add some cayenne pepper or smoked paprika to the meat mixture.
- Serve with a spicy mustard or Sriracha mayo dipping sauce.

Per Serving: Calories: 500; Total Fat: 26g; Saturated Fat: 7g; Cholesterol: 435mg; Sodium: 620mg; Total Carbs: 30g; Dietary Fiber: 2g; Total Sugars: 3g; Protein: 37g

Turkey Burgers

Servings: 4 | Prep Time: 10 Minutes | Cooking Time: 13 Minutes

Ingredients:

- 450g ground turkey
- 1/4 cup diced red onion
- 1 tablespoon grilled chicken seasoning
- 1/2 teaspoon dried parsley
- 1/2 teaspoon salt
- 4 slices provolone cheese
- 4 whole-grain sandwich buns
- Suggested toppings: lettuce, sliced tomatoes, dill pickles, and mustard

Directions:

1. Combine turkey, onion, seasoning, parsley and salt. Mix well.
2. Shape into 4 patties.
3. Cook at 180°C/360°F for 11 mins until turkey is

cooked through.
4. Top each burger with a cheese slice and cook 2 more mins to melt.
5. Serve on buns with desired toppings.

Variations & Ingredients Tips:

- Use ground chicken instead of turkey.
- Add breadcrumbs or an egg to bind the patties if too wet.
- Top with avocado, sauteed mushrooms or caramelized onions.

Per Serving: Calories: 299; Total Fat: 10g; Saturated Fat: 4g; Cholesterol: 95mg; Sodium: 726mg; Total Carbs: 25g; Dietary Fiber: 3g; Total Sugars: 3g; Protein: 31g

Chicken Chunks

Servings: 4 | Prep Time: 10 Minutes | Cooking Time: 10 Minutes

Ingredients:

- 450g chicken tenders cut into 4cm chunks
- Salt and pepper
- 1/2 cup cornstarch
- 2 eggs, beaten
- 1 cup panko breadcrumbs
- Oil for misting or cooking spray

Directions:

1. Season chicken chunks with salt and pepper.
2. Dip chicken in cornstarch, then egg, then panko crumbs to coat well.
3. Spray chicken chunks with oil on all sides.
4. Place in a single layer in air fryer basket. Cook at 200°C/390°F for 5 minutes.
5. Spray with more oil, flip chunks and cook 5 more minutes until golden and cooked through.
6. Repeat steps 4-5 for remaining chicken chunks.

Variations & Ingredients Tips:

- Use chicken breast or thigh meat instead of tenders.
- Add spices like paprika or cajun seasoning to the breadcrumb coating.
- Serve with ranch, honey mustard or bbq sauce for dipping.

Per Serving: Calories: 384; Total Fat: 8g; Saturated Fat: 2g; Cholesterol: 150mg; Sodium: 264mg; Total Carbs: 42g; Dietary Fiber: 2g; Total Sugars: 1g; Protein: 34g

Cal-mex Turkey Patties

Servings: 4 | Prep Time: 10 Minutes | Cooking Time: 30 Minutes

Ingredients:

- 1/3 cup crushed corn tortilla chips
- 1/3 cup grated American cheese
- 1 egg, beaten
- ¼ cup salsa
- Salt and pepper to taste
- 454 grams ground turkey
- 1 tbsp olive oil
- 1 tsp chili powder

Directions:

1. Preheat air fryer to 165°C/330°F.
2. Mix together egg, tortilla chips, salsa, cheese, salt, and pepper in a bowl.
3. Using your hands, add the ground turkey and mix gently until just combined.
4. Divide the meat into 4 equal portions and shape into patties about 1-cm thick.
5. Brush the patties with olive oil and sprinkle with chili powder.
6. Air Fry the patties for 14-16 minutes, flipping once until cooked through and golden.
7. Serve and enjoy!

Variations & Ingredients Tips:

- Use ground chicken or beef instead of turkey.
- Add diced jalapeños or green chiles to the patty mixture for extra heat.
- Serve on a bun with sliced avocado, tomato, and lettuce for a burger.

Per Serving: Calories: 330; Total Fat: 21g; Saturated Fat: 6g; Sodium: 470mg; Total Carbohydrates: 7g; Dietary Fiber: 1g; Total Sugars: 1g; Protein: 30g

Chicken Pigs In Blankets

Servings: 4 | Prep Time: 10 Minutes | Cooking Time: 40 Minutes

Ingredients:

- 8 chicken drumsticks, boneless, skinless
- 2 tbsp light brown sugar
- 2 tbsp ketchup

- 1 tbsp grainy mustard
- 8 smoked bacon slices
- 1 tsp chopped fresh sage

Directions:

1. Preheat the air fryer to 175°C/350°F.
2. Mix brown sugar, sage, ketchup, and mustard in a bowl and brush the chicken with it.
3. Wrap slices of bacon around the drumsticks and brush with the remaining mix.
4. Line the frying basket with round parchment paper with holes.
5. Set 4 drumsticks on the paper, add a raised rack and set the other drumsticks on it.
6. Bake for 25-35 minutes, moving the bottom drumsticks to the top, top to the bottom, and flipping at about 14-16 minutes.
7. Sprinkle with sage and serve.

Variations & Ingredients Tips:

- Use chicken thighs instead of drumsticks.
- Add a touch of hot sauce to the glaze for some heat.
- Wrap turkey bacon instead of pork bacon for a leaner option.

Per Serving (2 pigs in blankets): Calories: 296; Total Fat: 11g; Saturated Fat: 4g; Cholesterol: 114mg; Sodium: 832mg; Total Carbs: 18g; Dietary Fiber: 1g; Total Sugars: 10g; Protein: 31g

Sweet Nutty Chicken Breasts

Servings: 4 | Prep Time: 10 Minutes | Cooking Time: 30 Minutes

Ingredients:

- 2 chicken breasts, halved lengthwise
- 1/4 cup honey mustard
- 1/4 cup chopped pecans
- 1 tbsp olive oil
- 1 tbsp parsley, chopped

Directions:

1. Preheat air fryer to 175°C/350°F.
2. Brush chicken breasts with honey mustard and olive oil on all sides.
3. Place the pecans in a bowl. Add and coat the chicken breasts.
4. Place the breasts in the greased frying basket and Air Fry for 25 minutes, turning once.
5. Let chill onto a serving plate for 5 minutes. Sprinkle with parsley and serve.

Variations & Ingredients Tips:

- Use other nuts like almonds or walnuts instead of pecans.
- Add dried herbs like thyme or rosemary to the nut coating.
- Serve with a honey mustard dipping sauce on the side.

Per Serving: Calories: 307; Total Fat: 14g; Saturated Fat: 2g; Cholesterol: 88mg; Sodium: 237mg; Total Carbs: 14g; Dietary Fiber: 1g; Total Sugars: 10g; Protein: 31g

Windsor's Chicken Salad

Servings: 4 | Prep Time: 15 Minutes (plus Chilling Time) | Cooking Time: 30 Minutes

Ingredients:

- 1/2 cup halved seedless red grapes
- 2 chicken breasts, cubed
- Salt and pepper to taste
- 3/4 cup mayonnaise
- 1 tbsp lemon juice
- 2 tbsp chopped parsley
- 1/2 cup chopped celery
- 1 shallot, diced

Directions:

1. Preheat air fryer to 175°C/350°F.
2. Sprinkle chicken with salt and pepper. Place the chicken cubes in the frying basket and Air Fry for 9 minutes, flipping once.
3. In a salad bowl, combine the cooked chicken, mayonnaise, lemon juice, parsley, grapes, celery, and shallot and let chill covered in the fridge for 1 hour up to overnight.

Variations & Ingredients Tips:

- Add chopped toasted pecans or walnuts for crunch.
- Mix in some curry powder or Dijon mustard to the dressing.
- Serve in lettuce cups, sandwiches or wraps.

Per Serving: Calories: 470; Total Fat: 40g; Saturated Fat: 7g; Cholesterol: 95mg; Sodium: 380mg; Total Carbs: 6g; Dietary Fiber: 1g; Total Sugars: 4g; Protein: 24g

Daadi Chicken Salad

Servings: 2 | Prep Time: 20 Minutes | Cooking Time: 30 Minutes

Ingredients:

- 1/2 cup chopped golden raisins
- 1 Granny Smith apple, grated
- 2 chicken breasts
- Salt and pepper to taste
- 3/4 cup mayonnaise
- 1 tbsp lime juice
- 1 tsp curry powder
- 1/2 sliced avocado
- 1 scallion, minced
- 2 tbsp chopped pecans
- 1 tsp poppy seeds

Directions:

1. Preheat air fryer at 175°C/350°F.
2. Sprinkle chicken breasts with salt and pepper, place them in the greased frying basket, and Air Fry for 8-10 minutes, tossing once. Let rest for 5 minutes before cutting.
3. In a salad bowl, combine chopped chicken, mayonnaise, lime juice, curry powder, raisins, apple, avocado, scallion, and pecans. Let sit covered in the fridge until ready to eat.
4. Before serving, sprinkle with the poppy seeds.

Variations & Ingredients Tips:

- Substitute mayo with Greek yogurt for a lighter version.
- Add diced mango or pineapple for a fruity twist.
- Serve stuffed in pita pockets or on top of mixed greens.

Per Serving: Calories: 820; Total Fat: 63g; Saturated Fat: 9g; Cholesterol: 140mg; Sodium: 540mg; Total Carbs: 35g; Dietary Fiber: 7g; Total Sugars: 24g; Protein: 41g

Mexican Chicken Roll-ups

Servings: 4 | Prep Time: 15 Minutes | Cooking Time: 35 Minutes

Ingredients:

- 1/2 red bell pepper, cut into strips
- 1/2 green bell pepper, cut into strips
- 2 chicken breasts
- 1/2 lime, juiced
- 2 tbsp taco seasoning
- 1 spring onion, thinly sliced

Directions:

1. Preheat air fryer to 200°C/400°F.
2. Cut the chicken into cutlets by slicing the chicken breast in half horizontally in order to have 4 thin cutlets. Drizzle with lime juice and season with taco seasoning.
3. Divide the red pepper, green pepper, and spring onion equally between the 4 cutlets. Roll up the cutlets. Secure with toothpicks.
4. Place the chicken roll-ups in the air fryer and lightly spray with cooking oil. Bake for 12 minutes, turning once.
5. Serve warm.

Variations & Ingredients Tips:

- Add some shredded cheddar or pepper jack cheese inside the rolls.
- Serve with salsa, guacamole or sour cream for dipping.
- Use large lettuce leaves instead of bell peppers for a low-carb option.

Per Serving: Calories: 150; Total Fat: 3g; Saturated Fat: 0.5g; Cholesterol: 75mg; Sodium: 400mg; Total Carbs: 4g; Dietary Fiber: 1g; Total Sugars: 2g; Protein: 27g

Popcorn Chicken Tenders With Vegetables

Servings: 4 | Prep Time: 15 Minutes | Cooking Time: 30 Minutes

Ingredients:

- 2 tbsp cooked popcorn, ground
- Salt and pepper to taste
- 450g chicken tenders
- 1/2 cup bread crumbs
- 1/2 tsp dried thyme
- 1 tbsp olive oil
- 2 carrots, sliced
- 12 baby potatoes

Directions:

1. Preheat air fryer to 190°C/380°F.
2. Season the chicken tenders with salt and pepper.

3. In a shallow bowl, mix the crumbs, popcorn, thyme, and olive oil until combined. Coat the chicken with mixture. Press firmly, so the crumbs adhere.
4. Arrange the carrots and baby potatoes in the greased frying basket and top them with the chicken tenders.
5. Bake for 9-10 minutes. Shake the basket and continue cooking for another 9-10 minutes, until the vegetables are tender.
6. Serve and enjoy!

Variations & Ingredients Tips:

- Use crushed corn flakes or potato chips instead of popcorn.
- Add some garlic powder, paprika or parmesan to the breading.
- Serve with honey mustard, BBQ sauce or ranch for dipping.

Per Serving: Calories: 320; Total Fat: 9g; Saturated Fat: 1.5g; Cholesterol: 85mg; Sodium: 280mg; Total Carbs: 30g; Dietary Fiber: 3g; Total Sugars: 2g; Protein: 31g

Beef, Pork & Lamb Recipes

Sloppy Joes

Servings: 4 | Prep Time: 10 Minutes | Cooking Time: 17 Minutes

Ingredients:

- oil for misting or cooking spray
- 454 g very lean ground beef
- 1 teaspoon onion powder
- ⅓ cup ketchup
- ¼ cup water
- ½ teaspoon celery seed
- 1 tablespoon lemon juice
- 1½ teaspoons brown sugar
- 1¼ teaspoons low-sodium Worcestershire sauce
- ½ teaspoon salt (optional)
- ½ teaspoon vinegar
- ⅛ teaspoon dry mustard
- hamburger or slider buns

Directions:

1. Spray air fryer basket with nonstick cooking spray or olive oil.
2. Break raw ground beef into small chunks and pile into basket.
3. Cook at 195°C/390°F for 5 minutes. Stir to break apart and cook 3 minutes. Stir and cook 4 minutes longer or until meat is well done.
4. Remove meat from air fryer, drain, and use a knife and fork to crumble into small pieces.
5. Give your air fryer basket a quick rinse to remove any bits of meat.
6. Place all the remaining ingredients except the buns in a 15 x 15 cm baking pan and mix together.
7. Add meat and stir well.
8. Cook at 165°C/330°F for 5 minutes. Stir and cook for 2 minutes.
9. Scoop onto buns.

Variations & Ingredients Tips:

- Use ground turkey or chicken for a lighter version
- Add diced bell peppers, carrots or zucchini to the meat mixture for extra veggies
- Top with sliced cheese, pickles or coleslaw for crunch and flavor

Per Serving: Calories: 325; Total Fat: 15g; Saturated Fat: 5g; Cholesterol: 81mg; Sodium: 632mg; Total Carbs: 19g; Dietary Fiber: 1g; Total Sugars: 9g; Protein: 28g

Crispy Steak Subs

Servings: 2 | Prep Time: 10 Minutes | Cooking Time: 30 Minutes

Ingredients:

- 1 hoagie bun baguette, halved
- 170 g flank steak, sliced
- ½ white onion, sliced
- ½ red pepper, sliced
- 2 mozzarella cheese slices

Directions:

1. Preheat air fryer to 160°C/320°F.
2. Place the flank steak slices, onion, and red pepper on one side of the frying basket. Add the hoagie bun halves, crusty side up, to the other half of the air fryer.
3. Bake for 10 minutes. Flip the hoagie buns. Cover both sides with one slice of mozzarella cheese. Gently stir the steak, onions, and peppers.
4. Cook for 6 more minutes until the cheese is melted and the steak is juicy on the inside and crispy on the outside.
5. Remove the cheesy hoagie halves to a serving plate. Cover one side with the steak, and top with the onions and peppers. Close with the other cheesy hoagie half, slice into two pieces, and enjoy!

Variations & Ingredients Tips:

- Use different types of cheese, such as provolone or cheddar, for a variety of flavors.
- Add some sliced mushrooms or bell peppers to the steak mixture for extra vegetables.
- Serve the steak subs with a side of French fries or onion rings for a classic sandwich shop meal.

Per Serving: Calories: 510; Total Fat: 22g; Saturated Fat: 9g; Cholesterol: 75mg; Sodium: 770mg; Total Carbs: 45g; Fiber: 3g; Sugars: 6g; Protein: 35g

Classic Salisbury Steak Burgers

Servings: 4 | Prep Time: 15 Minutes | Cooking Time: 35 Minutes

Ingredients:

- ¼ cup bread crumbs
- 2 tablespoons beef broth
- 1 tablespoon cooking sherry
- 1 tablespoon ketchup
- 1 tablespoon Dijon mustard
- 2 teaspoons Worcestershire sauce
- ½ teaspoon onion powder
- ½ teaspoon garlic powder
- 450 g ground beef
- 1 cup sliced mushrooms
- 1 tablespoon butter
- 4 buns, split and toasted

Directions:

1. Preheat the air fryer to 190°C/375°F.
2. Combine the bread crumbs, broth, cooking sherry, ketchup, mustard, Worcestershire sauce, garlic and onion powder and mix well. Add the beef and mix with hands, then form into 4 patties and refrigerate while preparing the mushrooms.
3. Mix the mushrooms and butter in a 15 cm pan. Place the pan in the air fryer and Bake for 8-10 minutes, stirring once until the mushrooms are brown and tender. Remove and set aside.
4. Line the frying basket with round parchment paper and punch holes in it. Lay the burgers in a single layer and cook for 11-14 minutes or until cooked through.
5. Put the burgers on the bun bottoms, top with the mushrooms, then the bun tops.

Variations & Ingredients Tips:

- Use different types of mushrooms, such as shiitake or cremini, for a variety of flavors and textures.
- Add some sliced onions or bell peppers to the mushroom mixture for extra vegetables.
- Serve the Salisbury steak burgers with a side of mashed potatoes or green beans for a classic comfort food meal.

Per Serving: Calories: 430; Total Fat: 23g; Saturated Fat: 9g; Cholesterol: 105mg; Sodium: 670mg; Total Carbs: 26g; Fiber: 2g; Sugars: 5g; Protein: 31g

Pork Schnitzel With Dill Sauce

Servings: 4 | Prep Time: 20 Minutes | Cooking Time: 4 Minutes

Ingredients:

- 6 boneless, center cut pork chops (about 680 g)
- ½ cup flour
- 1½ teaspoons salt
- freshly ground black pepper
- 2 eggs
- ½ cup milk
- 1½ cups toasted fine breadcrumbs
- 1 teaspoon paprika

- 3 tablespoons butter, melted
- 2 tablespoons vegetable or olive oil
- lemon wedges
- Dill Sauce:
- 1 cup chicken stock
- 1½ tablespoons cornstarch
- ⅓ cup sour cream
- 1½ tablespoons chopped fresh dill
- salt and pepper

Directions:

1. Trim the excess fat from the pork chops and pound each chop with a meat mallet between two pieces of plastic wrap until they are 3 cm thick.
2. Set up a dredging station. Combine the flour, salt, and black pepper in a shallow dish. Whisk the eggs and milk together in a second shallow dish. Finally, combine the breadcrumbs and paprika in a third shallow dish.
3. Dip each flattened pork chop in the flour. Shake off the excess flour and dip each chop into the egg mixture. Finally dip them into the breadcrumbs and press the breadcrumbs onto the meat firmly. Place each finished chop on a baking sheet until they are all coated.
4. Preheat the air fryer to 200°C/400°F.
5. Combine the melted butter and the oil in a small bowl and lightly brush both sides of the coated pork chops. Do not brush the chops too heavily or the breading will not be as crispy.
6. Air-fry one schnitzel at a time for 4 minutes, turning it over halfway through the cooking time. Hold the cooked schnitzels warm on a baking pan in a 76°C/170°F oven while you finish air-frying the rest.
7. While the schnitzels are cooking, whisk the chicken stock and cornstarch together in a small saucepan over medium-high heat on the stovetop. Bring the mixture to a boil and simmer for 2 minutes. Remove the saucepan from heat and whisk in the sour cream. Add the chopped fresh dill and season with salt and pepper.
8. Transfer the pork schnitzel to a platter and serve with dill sauce and lemon wedges. For a traditional meal, serve this along side some egg noodles, spätzle or German potato salad.

Variations & Ingredients Tips:

- Use turkey cutlets or thin slices of eggplant for a change
- Add some Dijon mustard to the egg mixture for tangy flavor
- Garnish with capers, chopped parsley and sliced cucumbers

Per Serving: Calories: 662; Total Fat: 31g; Saturated Fat: 12g; Cholesterol: 238mg; Sodium: 1561mg; Total Carbs: 46g; Dietary Fiber: 2g; Total Sugars: 4g; Protein: 49g

Albóndigas

Servings: 4 | Prep Time: 10 Minutes | Cooking Time: 15 Minutes

Ingredients:

- 450 g lean ground pork
- 3 tablespoons very finely chopped trimmed scallions
- 3 tablespoons finely chopped fresh cilantro leaves
- 3 tablespoons plain panko bread crumbs (gluten-free, if a concern)
- 3 tablespoons dry white wine, dry sherry, or unsweetened apple juice
- 1½ teaspoons minced garlic
- 1¼ teaspoons mild smoked paprika
- ¾ teaspoon dried oregano
- ¾ teaspoon table salt
- ¼ teaspoon ground black pepper
- Olive oil spray

Directions:

1. Preheat the air fryer to 200°C/400°F.
2. Mix the ground pork, scallions, cilantro, bread crumbs, wine or its substitute, garlic, smoked paprika, oregano, salt, and pepper in a bowl until the herbs and spices are evenly distributed in the mixture.
3. Lightly coat your clean hands with olive oil spray, then form the ground pork mixture into balls, using 2 tablespoons for each one. Spray your hands frequently so that the meat mixture doesn't stick.
4. Set the balls in the basket so that they're not touching, even if they're close together. Air-fry undisturbed for 15 minutes, or until well browned and an instant-read meat thermometer inserted into one or two balls registers 75°C/165°F.
5. Use a nonstick-safe spatula and kitchen tongs for balance to gently transfer the fragile balls to a wire rack to cool for 5 minutes before serving.

Variations & Ingredients Tips:

- Use ground beef or lamb instead of pork for a different flavor profile.
- Add some finely chopped jalapeño or red pepper flakes to the meat mixture for a spicy kick.

- Serve the albóndigas with a dipping sauce, such as romesco or aioli, for extra flavor.

Per Serving: Calories: 290; Total Fat: 18g; Saturated Fat: 6g; Cholesterol: 85mg; Sodium: 550mg; Total Carbs: 7g; Fiber: 1g; Sugars: 1g; Protein: 25g

Skirt Steak With Horseradish Cream

Servings: 2 | Prep Time: 10 Minutes | Cooking Time: 20 Minutes

Ingredients:

- 1 cup heavy cream
- 3 tablespoons horseradish sauce
- 1 lemon, zested
- 1 skirt steak, halved
- 2 tablespoons olive oil
- Salt and pepper to taste

Directions:

1. Mix together the heavy cream, horseradish sauce, and lemon zest in a small bowl. Let chill in the fridge.
2. Preheat air fryer to 200°C/400°F. Brush steak halves with olive oil and sprinkle with salt and pepper. Place steaks in the frying basket and Air Fry for 10 minutes or until you reach your desired doneness, flipping once. Let sit onto a cutting board for 5 minutes. Thinly slice against the grain and divide between 2 plates. Drizzle with the horseradish sauce over. Serve and enjoy!

Variations & Ingredients Tips:

- Use sour cream or crème fraîche instead of heavy cream for a tangy twist
- Add some chopped chives or parsley to the sauce for freshness
- Serve with roasted potatoes, grilled asparagus or a simple salad

Per Serving: Calories: 738; Total Fat: 67g; Saturated Fat: 33g; Cholesterol: 174mg; Sodium: 262mg; Total Carbs: 7g; Dietary Fiber: 1g; Total Sugars: 4g; Protein: 31g

Flank Steak With Roasted Peppers And Chimichurri

Servings: 4 | Prep Time: 30 Minutes | Cooking Time: 22 Minutes

Ingredients:

- 2 cups flat-leaf parsley leaves
- ¼ cup fresh oregano leaves
- 3 cloves garlic
- ½ cup olive oil
- ¼ cup red wine vinegar
- ½ tsp salt
- freshly ground black pepper
- ¼ tsp crushed red pepper flakes
- ½ tsp ground cumin
- 454 g flank steak
- 1 red bell pepper, cut into strips
- 1 yellow bell pepper, cut into strips

Directions:

1. Make the chimichurri sauce by chopping the parsley, oregano and garlic in a food processor. Add the olive oil, vinegar and seasonings and process again. Pour half of the sauce into a shallow dish with the flank steak and set the remaining sauce aside. Pierce the flank steak with a needle-style meat tenderizer or a paring knife and marinate the steak for 2 to 24 hours in the refrigerator. When you are ready to cook, remove the steak from the refrigerator and let it sit at room temperature for 30 minutes.
2. Preheat the air fryer to 200°C/400°F.
3. Cut the flank steak in half so that it fits more easily into the air fryer and transfer both pieces to the air fryer basket. Air-fry for 14 minutes, depending on how you like your steak cooked (10 minutes will give you medium for a 2.5 cm thick flank steak). Flip the steak over halfway through the cooking time.
4. When the flank steak is cooked to your liking, transfer it to a cutting board, loosely tent with foil and let it rest while you cook the peppers.
5. Toss the peppers in a little olive oil, salt and freshly ground black pepper and transfer them to the air fryer basket. Air-fry at 200°C/400°F for 8 minutes, shaking the basket once or twice throughout the cooking process. To serve, slice the flank steak against the grain of the meat and top with the roasted peppers. Drizzle the reserved chimichurri sauce on top, thinning the sauce with another 1 tbsp of olive oil if desired.

Variations & Ingredients Tips:

- Reserve some of the raw bell peppers to add color and crunch to the final dish
- Add some sliced red onions to the peppers for extra flavor
- Chimichurri is also great on chicken, pork or seafood

41

Per Serving: Calories: 540; Total Fat: 43g; Saturated Fat: 9g; Cholesterol: 68mg; Sodium: 529mg; Total Carbs: 6g; Dietary Fiber: 2g; Total Sugars: 2g; Protein: 31g

Perfect Pork Chops

Servings: 3 | Prep Time: 5 Minutes | Cooking Time: 10 Minutes

Ingredients:

- ¾ teaspoon mild paprika
- ¾ teaspoon dried thyme
- ¾ teaspoon onion powder
- ¼ teaspoon garlic powder
- ¼ teaspoon table salt
- ¼ teaspoon ground black pepper
- 3 boneless center-cut pork loin chops (170 g each)
- Vegetable oil spray

Directions:

1. Preheat the air fryer to 200°C/400°F.
2. Mix the paprika, thyme, onion powder, garlic powder, salt, and pepper in a small bowl until well combined. Massage this mixture into both sides of the chops. Generously coat both sides of the chops with vegetable oil spray.
3. When the machine is at temperature, set the chops in the basket with as much air space between them as possible. Air-fry undisturbed for 10 minutes, or until an instant-read meat thermometer inserted into the thickest part of a chop registers 65°C/145°F.
4. Use kitchen tongs to transfer the chops to a cutting board or serving plates. Cool for 5 minutes before serving.

Variations & Ingredients Tips:

- Use different types of seasoning, such as Cajun or Italian, for a variety of flavors.
- Add some minced garlic or red pepper flakes to the seasoning mixture for extra flavor.
- Serve the pork chops with a side of roasted vegetables or mashed potatoes for a complete meal.

Per Serving: Calories: 260; Total Fat: 13g; Saturated Fat: 4g; Cholesterol: 105mg; Sodium: 300mg; Total Carbs: 1g; Fiber: 0g; Sugars: 0g; Protein: 35g

Grilled Pork & Bell Pepper Salad

Servings: 4 | Prep Time: 15 Minutes | Cooking Time: 25 Minutes

Ingredients:

- 1 cup sautéed button mushrooms, sliced
- 907 g pork tenderloin, sliced
- 1 tsp olive oil
- 1 tsp dried marjoram
- 6 tomato wedges
- 6 green olives
- 6 cups mixed salad greens
- 1 red bell pepper, sliced
- 1/3 cup vinaigrette dressing

Directions:

1. Preheat air fryer to 200°C/400°F. Combine the pork and olive oil, making sure the pork is well-coated. Season with marjoram. Lay the pork in the air fryer. Grill for 4-6 minutes, turning once until the pork is cooked through.
2. While the pork is cooking, toss the salad greens, red bell pepper, tomatoes, olives, and mushrooms into a bowl. Lay the pork slices on top of the salad, season with vinaigrette, and toss. Serve while the pork is still warm.

Variations & Ingredients Tips:

- Add some crumbled feta or goat cheese for a creamy tang
- Use baby spinach or arugula instead of mixed greens for a peppery kick
- Grill some red onion slices along with the pork for extra flavor

Per Serving: Calories: 405; Total Fat: 18g; Saturated Fat: 4g; Cholesterol: 147mg; Sodium: 289mg; Total Carbs: 8g; Dietary Fiber: 3g; Total Sugars: 4g; Protein: 53g

Pork Cutlets With Almond-lemon Crust

Servings: 3 | Prep Time: 15 Minutes | Cooking Time: 14 Minutes

Ingredients:

- ¾ cup Almond flour
- ¾ cup Plain dried bread crumbs (gluten-free,

- if a concern)
- 1½ teaspoons Finely grated lemon zest
- 1¼ teaspoons Table salt
- ¾ teaspoon Garlic powder
- ¾ teaspoon Dried oregano
- 1 Large egg white(s)
- 2 tablespoons Water
- 3 170 g center-cut boneless pork loin chops (about 2 cm thick)
- Olive oil spray

Directions:

1. Preheat the air fryer to 190°C/375°F.
2. Mix the almond flour, bread crumbs, lemon zest, salt, garlic powder, and dried oregano in a large bowl until well combined.
3. Whisk the egg white(s) and water in a shallow soup plate or small pie plate until uniform.
4. Dip a chop in the egg white mixture, turning it to coat all sides, even the ends. Let any excess egg white mixture slip back into the rest, then set it in the almond flour mixture. Turn it several times, pressing gently to coat it evenly. Generously coat the chop with olive oil spray, then set aside to dip and coat the remaining chop(s).
5. Set the chops in the basket with as much air space between them as possible. Air-fry undisturbed for 12 minutes, or until browned and crunchy. You may need to add 2 minutes to the cooking time if the machine is at 180°C/360°F.
6. Use kitchen tongs to transfer the chops to a wire rack. Cool for a few minutes before serving.

Variations & Ingredients Tips:

- Try using different nuts like pecans or hazelnuts in place of almonds
- Add some grated Parmesan cheese to the breading mixture for extra flavor
- Serve with a side of lemon wedges for squeezing over the cutlets

Per Serving: Calories: 499; Total Fat: 30g; Saturated Fat: 4g; Cholesterol: 116mg; Sodium: 1416mg; Total Carbs: 15g; Dietary Fiber: 4g; Total Sugars: 2g; Protein: 45g

Ground Beef Calzones

Servings: 6 | Prep Time: 20 Minutes | Cooking Time: 30 Minutes

Ingredients:

- 1 refrigerated pizza dough
- 1 cup shredded mozzarella
- ½ cup chopped onion
- 2 garlic cloves, minced
- ¼ cup chopped mushrooms
- 454 g ground beef
- 1 tbsp pizza seasoning
- Salt and pepper to taste
- 355 g marinara sauce
- 1 tsp flour

Directions:

1. Warm 1 tbsp of oil in a skillet over medium heat. Stir-fry onion, garlic and mushrooms for 2-3 minutes or until aromatic. Add beef, pizza seasoning, salt and pepper. Use a large spoon to break up the beef. Cook for 3 minutes or until brown. Stir in marinara sauce and set aside.
2. On a floured work surface, roll out pizza dough and cut into 6 equal-sized rectangles. On each rectangle, add ½ cup of beef and top with 1 tbsp of shredded cheese. Fold one side of the dough over the filling to the opposite side. Press the edges using the back of a fork to seal them. Preheat air fryer to 200°C/400°F. Place the first batch of calzones in the air fryer and spray with cooking oil. Bake for 10 minutes. Let cool slightly and serve warm.

Variations & Ingredients Tips:

- Use Italian sausage instead of ground beef for a spicier flavor
- Add some chopped pepperoni or ham to the filling
- Brush the calzones with garlic butter before air frying for extra richness

Per Serving: Calories: 481; Total Fat: 21g; Saturated Fat: 8g; Cholesterol: 77mg; Sodium: 912mg; Total Carbs: 44g; Dietary Fiber: 3g; Total Sugars: 6g; Protein: 30g

Beef Short Ribs

Servings: 4 | Prep Time: 10 Minutes | Cooking Time: 20 Minutes

Ingredients:

- 2 tbsp soy sauce
- 1 tbsp sesame oil
- 2 tbsp brown sugar
- 1 tsp ground ginger
- 2 garlic cloves, crushed

- 450 g beef short ribs

Directions:

1. In a small bowl, mix together the soy sauce, sesame oil, brown sugar, and ginger. Transfer the mixture to a large resealable plastic bag, and place the garlic cloves and short ribs into the bag. Secure and place in the refrigerator for an hour (or overnight). When you're ready to prepare the dish, preheat the air fryer to 165°C/330°F. Liberally spray the air fryer basket with olive oil mist and set the beef short ribs in the basket. Cook for 10 minutes, flip the short ribs, and then cook another 10 minutes. Remove the short ribs from the air fryer basket, loosely cover with aluminum foil, and let them rest. The short ribs will continue to cook after they're removed from the basket. Check the internal temperature after 5 minutes to make sure it reached 63°C/145°F if you prefer a well-done meat. If it didn't reach 63°C/145°F and you would like it to be cooked longer, you can put it back into the air fryer basket at 165°C/330°F for another 3 minutes. Remove from the basket and let it rest, covered with aluminum foil, for 5 minutes. Serve immediately.

Variations & Ingredients Tips:

- Add a splash of rice vinegar, mirin, or sake to the marinade for a Japanese-inspired flavor.
- Garnish with sliced scallions, sesame seeds, or chopped cilantro before serving.
- Serve with steamed rice, stir-fried vegetables, or kimchi for a complete Asian meal.

Per Serving: Calories: 414; Total Fat: 30g; Saturated Fat: 11g; Cholesterol: 98mg; Sodium: 628mg; Total Carbohydrates: 10g; Dietary Fiber: 0g; Total Sugars: 9g; Protein: 26g

Pork Schnitzel

Servings: 4 | Prep Time: 15 Minutes | Cooking Time: 14 Minutes

Ingredients:

- 4 boneless pork chops, pounded to 6 mm thickness
- 1 teaspoon salt, divided
- 1 teaspoon black pepper, divided
- ½ cup all-purpose flour
- 2 eggs
- 1 cup breadcrumbs
- ¼ teaspoon paprika
- 1 lemon, cut into wedges

Directions:

1. Season both sides of the pork chops with ½ teaspoon of the salt and ½ teaspoon of the pepper.
2. On a plate, place the flour.
3. In a large bowl, whisk the eggs.
4. In another large bowl, place the breadcrumbs.
5. Season the flour with the paprika and season the breadcrumbs with the remaining ½ teaspoon of salt and ½ teaspoon of pepper.
6. To bread the pork, place a pork chop in the flour, then into the whisked eggs, and then into the breadcrumbs. Place the breaded pork onto a plate and finish breading the remaining pork chops.
7. Preheat the air fryer to 200°C/390°F.
8. Place the pork chops into the air fryer, not overlapping and working in batches as needed. Spray the pork chops with cooking spray and cook for 8 minutes; flip the pork and cook for another 4 to 6 minutes or until cooked to an internal temperature of 63°C/145°F.
9. Serve with lemon wedges.

Variations & Ingredients Tips:

- Use chicken cutlets or thin slices of veal for variety
- Add some grated Parmesan cheese to the breadcrumbs for extra flavor
- Serve with German potato salad, sauerkraut or braised red cabbage

Per Serving: Calories: 368; Total Fat: 14g; Saturated Fat: 4g; Cholesterol: 167mg; Sodium: 813mg; Total Carbs: 27g; Dietary Fiber: 1g; Total Sugars: 2g; Protein: 34g

Wiener Schnitzel

Servings: 4 | Prep Time: 10 Minutes | Cooking Time: 14 Minutes

Ingredients:

- 4 thin boneless pork loin chops
- 2 tablespoons lemon juice
- 1/2 cup all-purpose flour
- 1 teaspoon salt
- 1/4 teaspoon marjoram
- 1 cup plain breadcrumbs
- 2 large eggs, beaten
- Oil for misting or cooking spray

Directions:

1. Rub the lemon juice into all sides of pork chops.
2. Mix together the flour, salt, and marjoram. Place flour mixture on a sheet of wax paper.
3. Place breadcrumbs on another sheet of wax paper.
4. Dip pork chops in flour, then beaten eggs, then breadcrumbs, coating both sides. Mist all sides with oil or cooking spray.
5. Spray air fryer basket with nonstick spray and place breaded pork chops in basket.
6. Cook at 198°C/390°F for 7 minutes. Turn chops, mist again with oil, and cook for another 7 minutes until well done.
7. Serve with lemon wedges.

Variations & Ingredients Tips:

- Use panko breadcrumbs instead of regular for extra crunch
- Add grated parmesan or lemon zest to the breadcrumb mixture
- Pound the pork chops thin if they are not thin-cut

Per Serving: Calories: 385; Total Fat: 10g; Saturated Fat: 2g; Cholesterol: 165mg; Sodium: 725mg; Total Carbs: 45g; Dietary Fiber: 1g; Total Sugars: 2g; Protein: 28g

Lamb Meatballs With Quick Tomato Sauce

Servings: 4 | Prep Time: 20 Minutes | Cooking Time: 8 Minutes

Ingredients:

- ½ small onion, finely diced
- 1 clove garlic, minced
- 450 g ground lamb
- 2 tablespoons fresh parsley, finely chopped (plus more for garnish)
- 2 teaspoons fresh oregano, finely chopped
- 2 tablespoons milk
- 1 egg yolk
- Salt and freshly ground black pepper
- ½ cup crumbled feta cheese, for garnish
- Tomato Sauce:
- 2 tablespoons butter
- 1 clove garlic, smashed
- Pinch crushed red pepper flakes
- ¼ teaspoon ground cinnamon
- 1 (800 g) can crushed tomatoes
- Salt, to taste

Directions:

1. Combine all ingredients for the meatballs in a large bowl and mix just until everything is combined. Shape the mixture into 4 cm balls or shape the meat between two spoons to make quenelles (little three-sided footballs).
2. Preheat the air fryer to 200°C/400°F.
3. While the air fryer is preheating, start the quick tomato sauce. Place the butter, garlic and red pepper flakes in a sauté pan and heat over medium heat on the stovetop. Let the garlic sizzle a little, but before the butter starts to brown, add the cinnamon and tomatoes. Bring to a simmer and simmer for 15 minutes. Season to taste with salt (but not too much as the feta that you will be sprinkling on at the end will be salty).
4. Brush the bottom of the air fryer basket with a little oil and transfer the meatballs to the air fryer basket in one layer, air-frying in batches if necessary.
5. Air-fry at 200°C/400°F for 8 minutes, giving the basket a shake once during the cooking process to turn the meatballs over.
6. To serve, spoon a pool of the tomato sauce onto plates and add the meatballs in a decorative manner. Sprinkle the feta cheese on top and garnish with more fresh parsley. Serve immediately.

Variations & Ingredients Tips:

- Use different types of cheese, such as goat cheese or Parmesan, for a variety of flavors.
- Add some chopped Kalamata olives or capers to the tomato sauce for a briny flavor.
- Serve the meatballs with a side of pasta or crusty bread for a complete meal.

Per Serving: Calories: 510; Total Fat: 38g; Saturated Fat: 18g; Cholesterol: 170mg; Sodium: 780mg; Total Carbs: 15g; Fiber: 3g; Sugars: 8g; Protein: 31g

Barbecue-style London Broil

Servings: 5 | Prep Time: 5 Minutes | Cooking Time: 17 Minutes

Ingredients:

- ¾ tsp mild smoked paprika
- ¾ tsp dried oregano
- ¾ tsp table salt
- ¾ tsp ground black pepper
- ¼ tsp garlic powder
- ¼ tsp onion powder

- 680 g beef London broil (in one piece)
- Olive oil spray

Directions:

1. Preheat the air fryer to 200°C/400°F. Mix the smoked paprika, oregano, salt, pepper, garlic powder, and onion powder in a small bowl until uniform. Pat and rub this mixture across all surfaces of the beef. Lightly coat the beef on all sides with olive oil spray. When the machine is at temperature, lay the London broil flat in the basket and air-fry undisturbed for 8 minutes for the small batch, 10 minutes for the medium batch, or 12 minutes for the large batch for medium-rare, until an instant-read meat thermometer inserted into the center of the meat registers 55°C/130°F (not USDA-approved). Add 1, 2, or 3 minutes, respectively (based on the size of the cut) for medium, until an instant-read meat thermometer registers 57°C/135°F (not USDA-approved). Or add 3, 4, or 5 minutes respectively for medium, until an instant-read meat thermometer registers 63°C/145°F (USDA-approved). Use kitchen tongs to transfer the London broil to a cutting board. Let the meat rest for 10 minutes. It needs a long time for the juices to be reincorporated into the meat's fibers. Carve it against the grain into very thin (less than 6-mm-thick) slices to serve.

Variations & Ingredients Tips:

- Marinate the beef in a mixture of soy sauce, Worcestershire sauce, olive oil, and garlic for extra flavor.
- Slice the cooked London broil and serve in sandwiches, salads, or wraps.
- Brush with chimichurri sauce or horseradish cream sauce before serving for a bright, tangy finish.

Per Serving: Calories: 213; Total Fat: 10g; Saturated Fat: 4g; Cholesterol: 74mg; Sodium: 416mg; Total Carbohydrates: 1g; Dietary Fiber: 0g; Total Sugars: 0g; Protein: 28g

Suwon Pork Meatballs

Servings: 4 | Prep Time: 15 Minutes | Cooking Time: 30 Minutes

Ingredients:

- 454 g ground pork
- 1 egg
- 1 teaspoon cumin
- 1 tablespoon gochujang
- 1 teaspoon tamari
- ¼ teaspoon ground ginger
- 59 g bread crumbs
- 1 scallion, sliced
- 60 g plum jam
- 1 teaspoon toasted sesame seeds

Directions:

1. Preheat air fryer at 175°C/350°F. In a bowl, combine all ingredients, except scallion greens, sesame seeds and plum jam. Form mixture into meatballs. Place meatballs in the greased frying basket and Air Fry for 8 minutes, flipping once. Garnish with scallion greens, plum jam and toasted sesame seeds to serve.

Variations & Ingredients Tips:

- Use ground beef, chicken or turkey instead of pork
- Add some grated carrot, zucchini or spinach to the mix for extra veggies
- Serve with steamed rice, kimchi and gochujang sauce

Per Serving: Calories: 378; Total Fat: 23g; Saturated Fat: 8g; Cholesterol: 131mg; Sodium: 440mg; Total Carbs: 18g; Dietary Fiber: 1g; Total Sugars: 7g; Protein: 26g

Meatloaf With Tangy Tomato Glaze

Servings: 6 | Prep Time: 20 Minutes | Cooking Time: 50 Minutes

Ingredients:

- 450 g ground beef
- 225 g ground pork
- 225 g ground veal (or turkey)
- 1 medium onion, diced
- 1 small clove of garlic, minced
- 2 egg yolks, lightly beaten
- 120 ml tomato ketchup
- 1 tablespoon Worcestershire sauce
- ½ cup plain breadcrumbs
- 2 teaspoons salt
- Freshly ground black pepper
- ½ cup chopped fresh parsley, plus more for garnish
- 6 tablespoons ketchup
- 1 tablespoon balsamic vinegar
- 2 tablespoons brown sugar

Directions:

1. Combine the meats, onion, garlic, egg yolks, ketchup, Worcestershire sauce, breadcrumbs, salt, pepper and fresh parsley in a large bowl and mix well.
2. Preheat the air fryer to 180°C/350°F and pour a little water into the bottom of the air fryer drawer. (This will help prevent the grease that drips into the bottom drawer from burning and smoking.)
3. Transfer the meatloaf mixture to the air fryer basket, packing it down gently. Run a spatula around the meatloaf to create a space about 1.25 cm wide between the meat and the side of the air fryer basket.
4. Air-fry at 180°C/350°F for 20 minutes. Carefully invert the meatloaf onto a plate (remember to remove the basket from the air fryer drawer so you don't pour all the grease out) and slide it back into the air fryer basket to turn it over. Re-shape the meatloaf with a spatula if necessary. Air-fry for another 20 minutes at 180°C/350°F.
5. Combine the ketchup, balsamic vinegar and brown sugar in a bowl and spread the mixture over the meatloaf. Air-fry for another 10 minutes, until an instant read thermometer inserted into the center of the meatloaf registers 70°C/160°F.
6. Allow the meatloaf to rest for a few more minutes and then transfer it to a serving platter using a spatula. Slice the meatloaf, sprinkle a little chopped parsley on top if desired, and serve.

Variations & Ingredients Tips:

- Use different types of breadcrumbs, such as panko or Italian-seasoned, for a variety of textures and flavors.
- Add some grated carrot or zucchini to the meatloaf mixture for extra moisture and nutrients.
- Serve the meatloaf with a side of mashed potatoes or roasted vegetables for a classic comfort food meal.

Per Serving: Calories: 440; Total Fat: 27g; Saturated Fat: 10g; Cholesterol: 155mg; Sodium: 1360mg; Total Carbs: 24g; Fiber: 1g; Sugars: 14g; Protein: 27g

Crunchy Veal Cutlets

Servings: 2 | Prep Time: 15 Minutes | Cooking Time: 5 Minutes

Ingredients:

- ½ cup all-purpose flour or tapioca flour
- 1 large egg(s), well beaten
- ¾ cup seasoned Italian-style dried bread crumbs (gluten-free, if a concern)
- 2 tablespoons yellow cornmeal
- 4 thinly pounded veal leg cutlets (55 g each, less than 6 mm thick)
- Olive oil spray

Directions:

1. Preheat the air fryer to 200°C/400°F.
2. Set up and fill three shallow soup plates or small pie plates on your counter: one for the flour; one for the egg(s); and one for the bread crumbs, whisked with the cornmeal until well combined.
3. Dredge a veal cutlet in the flour, coating it on both sides. Gently shake off any excess flour, then gently dip it in the beaten egg(s), coating both sides. Let the excess egg slip back into the rest. Dip the cutlet in the bread-crumb mixture, turning it several times and pressing gently to make an even coating on both sides. Coat it on both sides with olive oil spray, then set it aside and continue dredging and coating more cutlets.
4. When the machine is at temperature, set the cutlets in the basket so that they don't touch each other. Air-fry undisturbed for 5 minutes, or until crisp and brown. (If only some of the veal cutlets will fit in one layer for any selected batch—the sizes of air fryer baskets vary dramatically—work in batches as necessary.)
5. Use kitchen tongs to transfer the cutlets to a wire rack. Cool for only 1 to 2 minutes before serving.

Variations & Ingredients Tips:

- Use different types of breading, such as panko or crushed potato chips, for a variety of textures.
- Add some grated Parmesan cheese or nutritional yeast to the breadcrumb mixture for a cheesy flavor.
- Serve the veal cutlets with a side of tomato sauce or lemon wedges for a classic pairing.

Per Serving: Calories: 400; Total Fat: 13g; Saturated Fat: 3g; Cholesterol: 225mg; Sodium: 580mg; Total Carbs: 36g; Fiber: 2g; Sugars: 2g; Protein: 35g

Calf's Liver

Servings: 4 | Prep Time: 10 Minutes | Cooking Time: 5 Minutes

Ingredients:

- 450-g sliced calf's liver

- Salt and pepper
- 2 eggs
- 2 tablespoons milk
- 1/2 cup whole wheat flour
- 1 1/2 cups panko breadcrumbs
- 1/2 cup plain breadcrumbs
- 1/2 teaspoon salt
- 1/4 teaspoon pepper
- Oil for misting or cooking spray

Directions:

1. Cut liver slices crosswise into strips about 25cm wide. Sprinkle with salt and pepper to taste.
2. Beat together egg and milk in a shallow dish.
3. Place wheat flour in a second shallow dish.
4. In a third shallow dish, mix together panko, plain breadcrumbs, 1/2 teaspoon salt, and 1/4 teaspoon pepper.
5. Preheat air fryer to 390°F/199°C.
6. Dip liver strips in flour, egg wash, and then breadcrumbs, pressing in coating slightly to make crumbs stick.
7. Cooking half the liver at a time, place strips in air fryer basket in a single layer, close but not touching. Cook at 390°F/199°C for 5 minutes or until done to your preference.
8. Repeat step 7 to cook remaining liver.

Variations & Ingredients Tips:

- For extra crunch, use all panko breadcrumbs instead of a mix
- Add cayenne pepper or Cajun seasoning to the breadcrumb mix for a kick of flavor
- Serve with lemon wedges for squeezing over the cooked liver

Per Serving: Calories: 276; Total Fat: 8g; Saturated Fat: 2g; Cholesterol: 284mg; Sodium: 620mg; Total Carbs: 27g; Dietary Fiber: 2g; Total Sugars: 1g; Protein: 23g

Italian Stuffed Bell Peppers

Servings: 4 | Prep Time: 15 Minutes | Cooking Time: 35 Minutes

Ingredients:

- 1 link sweet Italian pork sausage (around 113g)
- 12 turkey pepperoni slices, halved
- 340g shredded mozzarella
- 4 red bell peppers
- 1 cup passata sauce
- 2 tbsp fresh basil, picked

Directions:

1. Preheat air fryer to 370°F/188°C. Bake sausage in the frying basket for 10 minutes, flipping once until cooked. Remove and let cool. Chop into 25cm pieces. Cut the peppers in half lengthwise. Remove the seeds and membranes. Reduce the air fryer temperature to 350°F/177°C. Put the peppers in the greased frying basket and Bake for 6-8 minutes, flipping once until just softened. Set aside.
2. Add 2 tbsp of passata to the pepper halves. Top with 3 tbsp of mozzarella, some sausage pieces, and 3 pepperoni halves. Sprinkle with basil. Place the stuffed peppers in the greased frying basket and Bake until the cheese has melted and the passata is warmed through, 7 minutes. Serve.

Variations & Ingredients Tips:

- Use ground Italian sausage instead of links for easier stuffing
- Add sauteed spinach or kale to the filling
- Top with grated parmesan before serving

Per Serving: Calories: 460; Total Fat: 28g; Saturated Fat: 12g; Cholesterol: 80mg; Sodium: 1160mg; Total Carbs: 28g; Dietary Fiber: 5g; Total Sugars: 12g; Protein: 28g

Fish And Seafood Recipes

Feta & Shrimp Pita

Servings: 4 | Prep Time: 10 Minutes | Cooking Time: 15 Minutes

Ingredients:

- 450g peeled shrimp, deveined
- 2 tbsp olive oil
- 1 tsp dried oregano
- 1/2 tsp dried thyme
- 1/2 tsp garlic powder
- 1/4 tsp shallot powder
- 1/4 tsp tarragon powder
- Salt and pepper to taste
- 4 whole-wheat pitas
- 115g feta cheese, crumbled
- 1 cup grated lettuce
- 1 tomato, diced
- 1/4 cup black olives, sliced
- 1 lemon

Directions:

1. Preheat oven to 195°C/380°F.
2. Mix shrimp with oil, oregano, thyme, garlic, shallot, tarragon powders, salt and pepper.
3. Pour shrimp in air fryer basket and bake 6-8 mins until cooked through.
4. Divide shrimp into warmed pitas with feta, lettuce, tomato, olives and lemon squeeze.
5. Serve and enjoy!

Variations & Ingredients Tips:

- Use cooked chicken instead of shrimp.
- Add sliced red onion or cucumber to the pita filling.
- Drizzle with tzatziki sauce instead of lemon juice.

Per Serving: Calories: 331; Total Fat: 14g; Saturated Fat: 4g; Cholesterol: 236mg; Sodium: 704mg; Total Carbs: 29g; Dietary Fiber: 4g; Total Sugars: 3g; Protein: 26g

Spiced Salmon Croquettes

Servings: 6 | Prep Time: 10 Minutes | Cooking Time: 20 Minutes

Ingredients:

- 1 (210g) can Alaskan pink salmon, bones removed
- 1 lime, zested
- 1 red chili, minced
- 2 tbsp cilantro, chopped
- 1 egg, beaten
- 1/2 cup bread crumbs
- 2 scallions, diced
- 1 tsp garlic powder
- Salt and pepper to taste

Directions:

1. Preheat air fryer to 200°C/400°F.
2. Mix salmon, egg, crumbs, scallions in a bowl.
3. Add garlic, lime zest, chili, cilantro, salt & pepper.
4. Divide into 6 portions and shape into patties.
5. Place patties in greased air fryer basket.
6. Air Fry 7 minutes, flip and cook 4 more mins until golden.
7. Serve.

Variations & Ingredients Tips:

- Use fresh or canned salmon.
- Add diced red bell pepper or jalapeño.
- Substitute panko crumbs for extra crunch.

Per Serving: Calories: 140; Total Fat: 4g; Saturated Fat: 1g; Cholesterol: 70mg; Sodium: 380mg; Total Carbs: 12g; Dietary Fiber: 1g; Sugars: 1g; Protein: 13g

Crispy Fish Sandwiches

Servings: 4 | Prep Time: 15 Minutes | Cooking Time: 25 Minutes

Ingredients:

- 1/2 cup torn iceberg lettuce
- 1/2 cup mayonnaise
- 1 tbsp Dijon mustard
- 1/2 cup diced dill pickles
- 1 tsp capers
- 1 tsp tarragon
- 1 tsp dill
- Salt and pepper to taste
- 1/3 cup flour
- 2 tbsp cornstarch
- 1 tsp smoked paprika
- 1/4 cup milk
- 1 egg
- 1/2 cup bread crumbs
- 4 cod fillets, cut in half
- 1 vine-ripe tomato, sliced
- 4 hamburger buns

Directions:

1. Mix the mayonnaise, mustard, pickles, capers, tarragon, dill, salt, and pepper in a small bowl and let the resulting tartare sauce chill covered in the fridge until ready to use.
2. Preheat air fryer at 190°C/375°F. In a bowl, mix the flour, cornstarch, paprika, and salt. In another bowl, beat the milk and egg and in a third bowl, add the breadcrumbs.
3. Roll the cod in the flour mixture, shake off excess flour. Then, dip in the egg, shake off excess egg. Finally, dredge in the breadcrumbs mixture.
4. Place fish pieces in the greased frying basket and Air Fry for 6 minutes, flipping once.
5. Add cooked fish, lettuce, tomato slices, and tartar sauce to each bottom bun and top with the top bun. Serve.

Variations & Ingredients Tips:

- Use haddock, pollack or catfish instead of cod.
- Add some hot sauce or cayenne to the tartar sauce for a spicy kick.
- Toast the buns before assembling for extra crunch.

Per Serving: Calories: 530; Total Fat: 28g; Saturated Fat: 5g; Cholesterol: 115mg; Sodium: 1050mg; Total Carbs: 46g; Dietary Fiber: 2g; Total Sugars: 8g; Protein: 29g

Crab Stuffed Salmon Roast

Servings: 4 | Prep Time: 15 Minutes | Cooking Time: 20 Minutes

Ingredients:

- 1 (680g) salmon fillet
- Salt and freshly ground black pepper
- 170g crabmeat
- 1 teaspoon finely chopped lemon zest
- 1 teaspoon Dijon mustard
- 1 tablespoon chopped fresh parsley, plus more for garnish
- 1 scallion, chopped
- 1/4 teaspoon salt
- Olive oil

Directions: | Prepare the salmon fillet by butterflying it. Slice into the thickest side of the salmon, parallel to the countertop and along the length of the fillet. Don't slice all the way through to the other side – stop about 2.5 cm from the edge. Open the salmon up like a book. Season the salmon with salt and freshly ground black pepper.

6. Make the crab filling by combining the crabmeat, lemon zest, mustard, parsley, scallion, salt and freshly ground black pepper in a bowl. Spread this filling in the center of the salmon. Fold one side of the salmon over the filling. Then fold the other side over on top.
7. Transfer the rolled salmon to the center of a piece of parchment paper that is roughly 15 cm wide and about 30 cm long. The parchment paper will act as a sling, making it easier to put the salmon into the air fryer. Preheat the air fryer to 190°C/370°F. Use the parchment paper to transfer the salmon roast to the air fryer basket and tuck the ends of the paper down beside the salmon. Drizzle a little olive oil on top and season with salt and pepper.
8. Air-fry the salmon at 190°C/370°F for 20 minutes.
9. Remove the roast from the air fryer and let it rest for a few minutes. Then, slice it, sprinkle some more lemon zest and parsley (or fresh chives) on top and serve.

Variations & Ingredients Tips:

- Use a blend of crab and shrimp for the stuffing.
- Add some finely diced red bell pepper to the filling for color.
- Serve with lemon wedges and a side of roasted asparagus.

Per Serving: Calories: 330; Total Fat: 19g; Saturated Fat: 3.5g; Cholesterol: 115mg; Sodium: 490mg; Total Carbs: 2g; Dietary Fiber: 0g; Total Sugars: 1g; Protein: 36g

Parmesan Fish Bites

Servings: 2 | Prep Time: 15 Minutes | Cooking

Time: 30 Minutes

Ingredients:

- 1 haddock fillet, cut into bite-sized pieces
- 1 tbsp shredded cheddar
- 2 tbsp shredded Parmesan
- 2 eggs, beaten
- 1/2 cup breadcrumbs
- Salt and pepper to taste
- 1/2 cup mayoracha sauce

Directions:

1. Preheat air fryer to 175°C/350°F.
2. Dip the fish strips in the beaten eggs.
3. Place the bread crumbs, Parmesan, cheddar, salt and pepper in a bowl and mix well.
4. Coat the fish strips in the dry mixture and place them on the foil-lined frying basket.
5. Air Fry for 14-16 minutes. Halfway through, shake the basket.
6. When done, the fish will be cooked through and crust golden brown.
7. Serve with mayoracha sauce for dipping and enjoy!

Variations & Ingredients Tips:

▶ Use cod, tilapia or other white fish.
▶ Substitute panko for regular breadcrumbs.
▶ Dip in ranch or tartar sauce instead of mayoracha.

Per Serving: Calories: 310; Total Fat: 10g; Saturated Fat: 4g; Cholesterol: 220mg; Sodium: 780mg; Total Carbs: 26g; Dietary Fiber: 1g; Sugars: 2g; Protein: 28g

Honey Pecan Shrimp

Servings: 4 | Prep Time: 15 Minutes | Cooking Time: 10 Minutes

Ingredients:

- 1/4 cup cornstarch
- 3/4 teaspoon sea salt, divided
- 1/4 teaspoon pepper
- 2 egg whites
- 2/3 cup finely chopped pecans
- 450g raw, peeled, and deveined shrimp
- 1/4 cup honey
- 2 tablespoons mayonnaise

Directions:

1. In a small bowl, whisk together the cornstarch, 1/2 teaspoon of the salt, and the pepper.
2. In a second bowl, whisk together the egg whites until soft and foamy. (They don't need to be whipped to peaks or even soft peaks, just frothy.)
3. In a third bowl, mix together the pecans and the remaining 1/4 teaspoon of sea salt.
4. Pat the shrimp dry with paper towels. Working in small batches, dip the shrimp into the cornstarch, then into the egg whites, and then into the pecans until all the shrimp are coated with pecans.
5. Preheat the air fryer to 165°C/330°F.
6. Place the coated shrimp inside the air fryer basket and spray with cooking spray. Cook for 5 minutes, toss the shrimp, and cook another 5 minutes.
7. Meanwhile, place the honey in a microwave-safe bowl and microwave for 30 seconds. Whisk in the mayonnaise until smooth and creamy. Pour the honey sauce into a serving bowl. Add the cooked shrimp to the serving bowl while hot and toss to coat.
8. Serve immediately.

Variations & Ingredients Tips:

▶ Use walnuts, almonds or panko instead of pecans.
▶ Add some cayenne or chili powder to the cornstarch for heat.
▶ Serve over a bed of greens with a citrus vinaigrette.

Per Serving: Calories: 390; Total Fat: 21g; Saturated Fat: 2g; Cholesterol: 230mg; Sodium: 990mg; Total Carbs: 29g; Dietary Fiber: 1g; Total Sugars: 20g; Protein: 27g

Sweet Potato-wrapped Shrimp

Servings: 3 | Prep Time: 15 Minutes | Cooking Time: 6 Minutes

Ingredients:

- 24 Long spiralized sweet potato strands
- Olive oil spray
- ¼ tsp garlic powder
- ¼ tsp table salt
- Up to a ⅛ tsp cayenne
- 12 Large shrimp (20–25 per g), peeled and deveined

Directions:

1. Preheat the air fryer to 200°C/400°F.
2. Lay the spiralized sweet potato strands on a large swath of paper towels and straighten out the strands to

long ropes. Coat them with olive oil spray, then sprinkle them with the garlic powder, salt, and cayenne.
3. Pick up 2 strands and wrap them around the center of a shrimp, with the ends tucked under what now becomes the bottom side of the shrimp. Continue wrapping the remainder of the shrimp.
4. Set the shrimp bottom side down in the basket with as much air space between them as possible. Air-fry undisturbed for 6 minutes, or until the sweet potato strands are crisp and the shrimp are pink and firm.
5. Use kitchen tongs to transfer the shrimp to a wire rack. Cool for only a minute or two before serving.

Variations & Ingredients Tips:

- Use zucchini noodles instead of sweet potato for a different flavor and texture.
- Add some paprika or chili powder to the seasoning mix for extra heat.
- Serve with a dipping sauce like sweet chili or garlic aioli.

Per Serving: Calories: 120; Total Fat: 1g; Saturated Fat: 0g; Cholesterol: 110mg; Sodium: 420mg; Total Carbohydrates: 12g; Dietary Fiber: 2g; Total Sugars: 3g; Protein: 14g

Chinese Fish Noodle Bowls

Servings: 4 | Prep Time: 25 Minutes | Cooking Time: 40 Minutes

Ingredients:

- 1 can crushed pineapple, drained
- 1 shallot, minced
- 2 tbsp chopped cilantro
- 2 1/2 tsp lime juice
- 1 tbsp honey
- Salt and pepper to taste
- 1 1/2 cups grated red cabbage
- 1/4 cup chopped green beans
- 2 grated baby carrots
- 1/2 tsp granulated sugar
- 2 tbsp mayonnaise
- 1 clove garlic, minced
- 225g cooked rice noodles
- 2 tsp sesame oil
- 1 tsp sesame seeds
- 4 cod fillets
- 1 tsp Chinese five-spice

Directions:

1. Preheat air fryer at 175°C/350°F.
2. Combine the pineapple, shallot, 1 tbsp of cilantro, honey, 2 tsp of lime juice, salt, and black pepper in a bowl. Let chill the salsa covered in the fridge until ready to use.
3. Mix the cabbage, green beans, carrots, sugar, remaining lime juice, mayonnaise, garlic, salt, and pepper in a bowl. Let chill covered in the fridge until ready to use.
4. In a bowl, toss cooked noodles and sesame oil, stirring occasionally to avoid sticking.
5. Sprinkle cod fillets with salt and five-spice. Place them in the greased frying basket and Air Fry for 10 minutes until the fish is opaque and flakes easily with a fork.
6. Divide noodles into 4 bowls, top each with salsa, slaw, and fish. Serve right away sprinkled with another tbsp of cilantro and sesame seeds.

Variations & Ingredients Tips:

- Use salmon, shrimp or tofu instead of cod.
- Add some sliced mango or papaya to the salsa.
- Drizzle with a spicy Sriracha mayo sauce.

Per Serving: Calories: 400; Total Fat: 13g; Saturated Fat: 2g; Cholesterol: 65mg; Sodium: 330mg; Total Carbs: 45g; Dietary Fiber: 4g; Total Sugars: 18g; Protein: 27g

Lemon-dill Salmon Burgers

Servings: 4 | Prep Time: 15 Minutes | Cooking Time: 8 Minutes

Ingredients:

- 2 (170g) fillets of salmon, finely chopped by hand or in a food processor
- 1 cup fine breadcrumbs
- 1 teaspoon freshly grated lemon zest
- 2 tablespoons chopped fresh dill weed
- 1 teaspoon salt
- Freshly ground black pepper
- 2 eggs, lightly beaten
- 4 brioche or hamburger buns
- Lettuce, tomato, red onion, avocado, mayonnaise or mustard, to serve

Directions:

1. Preheat the air fryer to 200°C/400°F.
2. Combine all the ingredients in a bowl. Mix together well and divide into four balls. Flatten the balls into patties, making an indentation in the center of each patty with your thumb (this will help the burger stay

flat as it cooks) and flattening the sides of the burgers so that they fit nicely into the air fryer basket.
3. Transfer the burgers to the air fryer basket and air-fry for 4 minutes. Flip the burgers over and air-fry for another 3 to 4 minutes, until nicely browned and firm to the touch.
4. Serve on soft brioche buns with your choice of topping – lettuce, tomato, red onion, avocado, mayonnaise or mustard.

Variations & Ingredients Tips:

- Use canned salmon or tuna instead of fresh for convenience.
- Add some capers, olives or sun-dried tomatoes to the burger mix.
- Top with a tangy tzatziki sauce or spicy remoulade.

Per Serving: Calories: 430; Total Fat: 22g; Saturated Fat: 4.5g; Cholesterol: 170mg; Sodium: 890mg; Total Carbs: 32g; Dietary Fiber: 2g; Total Sugars: 5g; Protein: 28g

Almond-crusted Fish

Servings: 4 | Prep Time: 15 Minutes | Cooking Time: 10 Minutes

Ingredients:

- 4 (115-g) fish fillets
- 3/4 cup breadcrumbs
- 1/4 cup sliced almonds, crushed
- 2 tablespoons lemon juice
- 1/8 teaspoon cayenne
- Salt and pepper
- 3/4 cup flour
- 1 egg, beaten with 1 tablespoon water
- Oil for misting or cooking spray

Directions:

1. Split fish fillets lengthwise down the center to create 8 pieces.
2. Mix breadcrumbs and almonds together and set aside.
3. Mix the lemon juice and cayenne together. Brush on all sides of fish.
4. Season fish to taste with salt and pepper.
5. Place the flour on a sheet of wax paper.
6. Roll fillets in flour, dip in egg wash, and roll in the crumb mixture.
7. Mist both sides of fish with oil or cooking spray.
8. Spray air fryer basket and lay fillets inside.
9. Cook at 200°C/390°F for 5 minutes, turn fish over, and cook for an additional 5 minutes or until fish is done and flakes easily.

Variations & Ingredients Tips:

- Use panko breadcrumbs for extra crunch.
- Substitute almonds with pecans, walnuts or pistachios.
- Serve with tartar sauce and lemon wedges.

Per Serving: Calories: 270; Total Fat: 9g; Saturated Fat: 1.5g; Cholesterol: 110mg; Sodium: 320mg; Total Carbs: 22g; Dietary Fiber: 2g; Total Sugars: 1g; Protein: 25g

Garlic And Dill Salmon

Servings: 2 | Prep Time: 10 Minutes | Cooking Time: 8 Minutes

Ingredients:

- 340g salmon fillets with skin
- 2 tablespoons melted butter
- 1 tablespoon extra-virgin olive oil
- 2 garlic cloves, minced
- 1 tablespoon fresh dill
- 1/2 teaspoon sea salt
- 1/2 lemon

Directions:

1. Pat the salmon dry with paper towels.
2. Mix together melted butter, olive oil, garlic, and dill.
3. Sprinkle salmon with sea salt. Brush all sides with garlic-dill butter.
4. Preheat air fryer to 175°C/350°F.
5. Place salmon skin-side down in air fryer basket. Cook 6-8 mins until fish flakes.
6. Remove and squeeze fresh lemon over top. Serve immediately.

Variations & Ingredients Tips:

- Use different fresh herbs like parsley or thyme.
- Add lemon zest or white wine to the butter sauce.
- Serve over a salad or with roasted vegetables.

Per Serving: Calories: 367; Total Fat: 26g; Saturated Fat: 9g; Cholesterol: 109mg; Sodium: 401mg; Total Carbs: 1g; Dietary Fiber: 0g; Total Sugars: 0g; Protein: 33g

Cajun-seasoned Shrimp

Servings: 2 | Prep Time: 5 Minutes | Cooking Time: 15 Minutes

Ingredients:

- 454 grams shelled tail on shrimp, deveined
- 2 tsp grated Parmesan cheese
- 2 tbsp butter, melted
- 1 tsp cayenne pepper
- 1 tsp garlic powder
- 2 tsp Cajun seasoning
- 1 tbsp lemon juice

Directions:

1. Preheat air fryer at 180°C/350°F.
2. Toss the shrimp, melted butter, cayenne pepper, garlic powder and cajun seasoning in a bowl, place them in the greased air fryer basket, and Air Fry for 6 minutes, flipping once.
3. Transfer it to a plate. Squeeze lemon juice over shrimp and stir in Parmesan cheese.
4. Serve immediately.

Variations & Ingredients Tips:

- Use peeled, deveined shrimp with or without tails for easier eating.
- Add a dash of hot sauce or red pepper flakes for extra heat.
- Serve over rice, pasta, or in tacos or po' boy sandwiches.

Per Serving: Calories: 400; Total Fat: 22g; Saturated Fat: 12g; Sodium: 2040mg; Total Carbohydrates: 4g; Dietary Fiber: 1g; Total Sugars: 0g; Protein: 45g

Shrimp Teriyaki

Servings: 10 | Prep Time: 10 Minutes | Cooking Time: 6 Minutes

Ingredients:

- 1 tablespoon Regular or low-sodium soy sauce or gluten-free tamari sauce
- 1 tablespoon Mirin or substitute
- 1 teaspoon Ginger juice
- 10 Large shrimp, peeled and deveined
- 2/3 cup Plain panko bread crumbs
- 1 Large egg
- Vegetable oil spray

Directions:

1. Whisk soy sauce, mirin, and ginger juice in a pan. Add shrimp and toss to coat. Cover and refrigerate 1 hour, tossing shrimp periodically.
2. Preheat air fryer to 200°C/400°F.
3. Thread marinated shrimp onto 10-cm skewers, leaving space between each.
4. Pour breadcrumbs onto a plate. Whisk egg in pan with remaining marinade.
5. Dip skewered shrimp in egg mix, then coat in breadcrumbs, pressing gently. Spray with oil.
6. Place skewers in single layer in air fryer basket. Air-fry 6 minutes until pink and firm.
7. Transfer to a rack and let cool briefly before serving.

Variations & Ingredients Tips:

- Use coconut panko or crushed cornflakes instead of regular breadcrumbs.
- Brush shrimp with teriyaki glaze after cooking.
- Serve over rice or salad greens.

Per Serving: Calories: 100; Total Fat: 2g; Saturated Fat: 1g; Cholesterol: 90mg; Sodium: 270mg; Total Carbs: 10g; Dietary Fiber: 0g; Sugars: 1g; Protein: 10g

Almond Topped Trout

Servings: 4 | Prep Time: 5 Minutes | Cooking Time: 20 Minutes

Ingredients:

- 4 trout fillets
- 2 tbsp olive oil
- Salt and pepper to taste
- 2 garlic cloves, sliced
- 1 lemon, sliced
- 1 tbsp flaked almonds

Directions:

1. Preheat air fryer to 190°C/380°F.
2. Lightly brush each fillet with olive oil on both sides and season with salt and pepper.
3. Put the fillets in a single layer in the frying basket. Put the sliced garlic over the tops of the trout fillets, then top with lemon slices and cook for 12-15 minutes.
4. Serve topped with flaked almonds and enjoy!

Variations & Ingredients Tips:

- Use cod, haddock or snapper fillets instead of trout.
- Add dried herbs like dill, thyme or oregano to the seasoning.
- Drizzle with a lemon-caper sauce before serving.

Per Serving: Calories: 280; Total Fat: 18g; Saturated Fat: 3g; Cholesterol: 75mg; Sodium: 140mg; Total Carbs: 2g; Dietary Fiber: 1g; Total Sugars: 0g; Protein: 28g

Old Bay Lobster Tails

Servings: 2 | Prep Time: 10 Minutes | Cooking Time: 20 Minutes

Ingredients:

- 1/4 cup green onions, sliced
- 2 uncooked lobster tails
- 1 tbsp butter, melted
- 1/2 tsp Old Bay Seasoning
- 1 tbsp chopped parsley
- 1 tsp dried sage
- 1 tsp dried thyme
- 1 garlic clove, chopped
- 1 tbsp basil paste
- 2 lemon wedges

Directions:

1. Preheat air fryer at 200°C/400°F.
2. Using kitchen shears, cut down the middle of each lobster tail on the softer side. Carefully loosen the meat.
3. Place tails, cut side-up, in the frying basket and Air Fry for 4 minutes.
4. Brush tail meat with butter and season with Old Bay, sage, thyme, garlic, green onions, basil paste and cook 4 more minutes.
5. Scatter with parsley and serve with lemon wedges. Enjoy!

Variations & Ingredients Tips:

- Stuff the tail cavity with breadcrumb stuffing before cooking.
- Brush tails with garlic butter or herb butter.
- Drizzle with melted lemon butter when done.

Per Serving: Calories: 280; Total Fat: 11g; Saturated Fat: 5g; Cholesterol: 220mg; Sodium: 910mg; Total Carbs: 5g; Dietary Fiber: 1g; Sugars: 1g; Protein: 39g

Yummy Salmon Burgers With Salsa Rosa

Servings: 4 | Prep Time: 20 Minutes | Cooking Time: 35 Minutes + Chilling Time

Ingredients:

- 1/4 cup minced red onion
- 1/4 cup slivered onions
- 1/2 cup mayonnaise
- 2 tsp ketchup
- 1 tsp brandy
- 2 tsp orange juice
- 450g salmon fillets
- 5 tbsp panko bread crumbs
- 1 garlic clove, minced
- 1 large egg, lightly beaten
- 1 tbsp Dijon mustard
- 1 tsp fresh lemon juice
- 1 tbsp chopped parsley
- Salt to taste
- 4 buns
- 8 Boston lettuce leaves

Directions:

1. Mix the mayonnaise, ketchup, brandy, and orange juice in a bowl until blended. Set aside the resulting salsa rosa until ready to serve.
2. Cut a 115g section of salmon and place in a food processor. Pulse until it turns into a paste. Chop the remaining salmon into cubes and transfer to a bowl along with the salmon paste.
3. Add the panko, minced onion, garlic, egg, mustard, lemon juice, parsley, and salt. Toss to combine. Divide into 5 patties about 2-cm thick. Refrigerate for 30 minutes.
4. Preheat air fryer to 200°C/400°F. Place the patties in the greased frying basket. Air Fry for 12-14 minutes, flipping once until golden.
5. Serve each patty on a bun, 2 lettuce leaves, 2 tbsp of salsa rosa, and slivered onions. Enjoy!

Variations & Ingredients Tips:

- Use canned salmon instead of fresh for convenience.
- Add some diced bell peppers or jalapeños to the burger mix.
- Top with sliced avocado and crispy bacon.

Per Serving: Calories: 540; Total Fat: 34g; Saturated Fat: 6g; Cholesterol: 140mg; Sodium: 830mg; Total Carbs: 30g; Dietary Fiber: 2g; Total Sugars: 6g; Protein: 32g

Southern Shrimp With Cocktail Sauce

Servings: 2 | Prep Time: 15 Minutes | Cooking Time: 20 Minutes

Ingredients:

- 225g raw shrimp, tail-on, deveined and shelled
- 1 cup ketchup
- 2 tbsp prepared horseradish
- 1 tbsp lemon juice
- 1/2 tsp Worcestershire sauce
- 1/8 tsp chili powder
- Salt and pepper to taste
- 1/3 cup flour
- 2 tbsp cornstarch
- 1/4 cup milk
- 1 egg
- 1/2 cup bread crumbs
- 1 tbsp Cajun seasoning
- 1 lemon, cut into pieces

Directions:

1. Make cocktail sauce by whisking ketchup, horseradish, lemon, Worcestershire, chili, salt and pepper. Chill until ready.
2. Preheat air fryer at 190°C/375°F.
3. In one bowl, mix flour, cornstarch and salt. In another, beat milk and egg. In third bowl, mix breadcrumbs and Cajun seasoning.
4. Dredge shrimp in flour, dip in egg, then coat in breadcrumb mixture.
5. Place shrimp in greased air fryer basket. Air Fry 8 minutes, flipping once.
6. Serve hot shrimp with chilled cocktail sauce and lemon wedges.

Variations & Ingredients Tips:

- For spicier sauce, add hot sauce or horseradish.
- Substitute panko breadcrumbs for extra crunch.
- Serve shrimp over a salad instead of as an appetizer.

Per Serving: Calories: 475; Total Fat: 9g; Saturated Fat: 2g; Cholesterol: 200mg; Sodium: 1370mg; Total Carbs: 70g; Dietary Fiber: 4g; Sugars: 16g; Protein: 28g

Corn & Shrimp Boil

Servings: 4 | Prep Time: 15 Minutes | Cooking Time: 40 Minutes

Ingredients:

- 8 frozen "mini" corn on the cob
- 1 tbsp smoked paprika
- 2 tsp dried thyme
- 1 tsp dried marjoram
- 1 tsp sea salt
- 1 tsp garlic powder
- 1 tsp onion powder
- 1 tsp cayenne pepper
- 450g baby potatoes, halved
- 1 tbsp olive oil
- 450g peeled shrimp, deveined
- 1 avocado, sliced

Directions:

1. Preheat the air fryer to 190°C/370°F.
2. Combine the paprika, thyme, marjoram, salt, garlic, onion, and cayenne and mix well. Pour into a small glass jar.
3. Add the potatoes, corn, and olive oil to the frying basket and sprinkle with 2 tsp of the spice mix and toss. Air Fry for 15 minutes, shaking the basket once until tender. Remove and set aside.
4. Put the shrimp in the frying basket and sprinkle with 2 tsp of the spice mix. Air Fry for 5-8 minutes, shaking once until shrimp are tender and pink.
5. Combine all the ingredients in the frying basket and sprinkle with 2 tsp of the spice mix. Toss to coat and cook for 1-2 more minutes or until hot.
6. Serve topped with avocado.

Variations & Ingredients Tips:

- Add some sliced andouille sausage or bacon to the mix.
- Squeeze some lemon juice over the top before serving.
- Sprinkle with chopped fresh parsley or dill.

Per Serving: Calories: 380; Total Fat: 16g; Saturated Fat: 2.5g; Cholesterol: 180mg; Sodium: 1220mg; Total Carbs: 40g; Dietary Fiber: 8g; Total Sugars: 5g; Protein: 27g

Lemon-roasted Salmon Fillets

Servings: 3 | Prep Time: 5 Minutes | Cooking

Time: 7 Minutes

Ingredients:

- 3 (170g) skin-on salmon fillets
- Olive oil spray
- 9 very thin lemon slices
- 3/4 teaspoon ground black pepper
- 1/4 teaspoon table salt

Directions:

1. Preheat the air fryer to 200°C/400°F.
2. Generously coat the skin of each of the fillets with olive oil spray. Set the fillets skin side down on your work surface. Place three overlapping lemon slices down the length of each salmon fillet. Sprinkle them with the pepper and salt. Coat lightly with olive oil spray.
3. Use a nonstick-safe spatula to transfer the fillets one by one to the basket, leaving as much air space between them as possible. Air-fry undisturbed for 7 minutes, or until cooked through.
4. Use a nonstick-safe spatula to transfer the fillets to serving plates. Cool for only a minute or two before serving.

Variations & Ingredients Tips:

- Use lime, orange or grapefruit slices instead of lemon.
- Sprinkle with dill, parsley or chives before air frying.
- Serve over a bed of quinoa, couscous or cauliflower rice.

Per Serving: Calories: 280; Total Fat: 16g; Saturated Fat: 3g; Cholesterol: 95mg; Sodium: 260mg; Total Carbs: 2g; Dietary Fiber: 1g; Total Sugars: 0g; Protein: 32g

Mediterranean Sea Scallops

Servings: 2 | Prep Time: 15 Minutes | Cooking Time: 20 Minutes

Ingredients:

- 1 tbsp olive oil
- 1 shallot, minced
- 2 tbsp capers
- 2 cloves garlic, minced
- 1/2 cup heavy cream
- 3 tbsp butter
- 1 tbsp lemon juice
- Salt and pepper to taste
- 1/4 tbsp cumin powder
- 1/4 tbsp curry powder
- 450g jumbo sea scallops
- 2 tbsp chopped parsley
- 1 tbsp chopped cilantro

Directions:

1. Warm the olive oil in a saucepan over medium heat. Add shallot and stir-fry for 2 minutes until translucent.
2. Stir in capers, cumin, curry, garlic, heavy cream, 1 tbsp butter, lemon juice, salt and pepper and cook for 2 minutes until boiling. Lower heat and simmer 3 minutes until sauce thickens. Turn off heat.
3. Preheat air fryer at 200°C/400°F.
4. In a bowl, add remaining 2 tbsp butter and scallops and toss to coat all sides.
5. Place scallops in greased frying basket and Air Fry for 8 minutes, flipping once.
6. Drizzle caper sauce over, scatter with parsley, cilantro and serve.

Variations & Ingredients Tips:

- Use bay scallops instead of jumbo.
- Add white wine or vegetable broth to the sauce.
- Serve over linguine or zucchini noodles.

Per Serving: Calories: 430, Total Fat: 32g, Saturated Fat: 16g, Cholesterol: 135mg, Sodium: 590mg, Total Carbs: 10g, Fiber: 1g, Sugars: 2g, Protein: 28g

Tilapia Teriyaki

Servings: 3 | Prep Time: 10 Minutes | Cooking Time: 10 Minutes

Ingredients:

- 4 tablespoons teriyaki sauce
- 1 tablespoon pineapple juice
- 450g tilapia fillets
- Cooking spray
- 170g frozen mixed peppers with onions, thawed and drained
- 2 cups cooked rice

Directions:

1. Mix the teriyaki sauce and pineapple juice together in a small bowl.
2. Split tilapia fillets down the center lengthwise.
3. Brush all sides of fish with the sauce, spray air fryer basket with nonstick cooking spray, and place fish in the basket.

4. Stir the peppers and onions into the remaining sauce and spoon over the fish. Save any leftover sauce for drizzling over the fish when serving.
5. Cook at 180°C/360°F for 10 minutes, until fish flakes easily with a fork and is done in center.
6. Divide into 3 or 4 servings and serve each with approximately 120ml/1/2 cup cooked rice.

Variations & Ingredients Tips:

▶ Use salmon, cod or halibut instead of tilapia.
▶ Add some diced pineapple or mango to the veggies.
▶ Sprinkle with toasted sesame seeds and sliced scallions before serving.

Per Serving: Calories: 290; Total Fat: 4g; Saturated Fat: 1g; Cholesterol: 85mg; Sodium: 810mg; Total Carbs: 34g; Dietary Fiber: 2g; Total Sugars: 9g; Protein: 30g

Vegetarian Recipes

Lentil Fritters

Servings: 9 | Prep Time: 10 Minutes | Cooking Time: 12 Minutes

Ingredients:

- 1 cup cooked red lentils
- 1 cup riced cauliflower
- ½ medium zucchini, shredded (about 1 cup)
- ¼ cup finely chopped onion
- ¼ teaspoon salt
- ¼ teaspoon black pepper
- ½ teaspoon garlic powder
- ¼ teaspoon paprika
- 1 large egg
- ⅓ cup quinoa flour

Directions:

1. Preheat the air fryer to 190°C/370°F.
2. In a large bowl, mix the lentils, cauliflower, zucchini, onion, salt, pepper, garlic powder, and paprika. Mix in the egg and flour until a thick dough forms.
3. Using a large spoon, form the dough into 9 large fritters.
4. Liberally spray the air fryer basket with olive oil. Place the fritters into the basket, leaving space around each fritter so you can flip them.
5. Cook for 6 minutes, flip, and cook another 6 minutes.
6. Remove from the air fryer and repeat with the remaining fritters. Serve warm with desired sauce and sides.

Variations & Ingredients Tips:

▶ Use chickpea flour or almond meal instead of quinoa flour for a different flavor.
▶ Add shredded carrots or chopped bell peppers for extra veggie goodness.
▶ Serve with yogurt dip, hummus, or sweet chili sauce.

Per Serving: Calories: 60; Total Fat: 1.5g; Saturated Fat: 0g; Sodium: 90mg; Total Carbohydrates: 8g; Dietary Fiber: 2g; Total Sugars: 1g; Protein: 3g

Pinto Bean Casserole

Servings: 2 | Prep Time: 5 Minutes | Cooking Time: 15 Minutes

Ingredients:

- 1 can pinto beans
- ¼ cup tomato sauce
- 2 tbsp cornstarch
- 2 garlic cloves, minced
- ½ tsp dried oregano
- ½ tsp cumin
- 1 tsp smoked paprika
- Salt and pepper to taste

Directions:

1. Preheat air fryer to 200°C/390°F.
2. Stir the beans, tomato sauce, cornstarch, garlic, oregano, cumin, smoked paprika, salt, and pepper in a bowl until combined.
3. Pour the bean mix into a greased baking pan.
4. Bake in the fryer for 4 minutes. Remove, stir, and Bake for 4 minutes or until the mix is thick and heated through.
5. Serve hot.

Variations & Ingredients Tips:

- Top with shredded cheese, sour cream, and chopped cilantro.
- Add diced bell peppers and onions for extra veggies.
- Use black beans or kidney beans for variation.

Per Serving: Calories: 280; Total Fat: 1.5g; Saturated Fat: 0g; Sodium: 980mg; Total Carbohydrates: 52g; Dietary Fiber: 15g; Total Sugars: 2g; Protein: 15g

Lentil Burritos With Cilantro Chutney

Servings: 4 | Prep Time: 20 Minutes | Cooking Time: 30 Minutes

Ingredients:

- 1 cup cilantro chutney
- 454 grams cooked potatoes, mashed
- 2 tsp sunflower oil
- 3 garlic cloves, minced
- 1 ½ tbsp fresh lime juice
- 1 ½ tsp cumin powder
- 1 tsp onion powder
- 1 tsp coriander powder
- Salt to taste
- ½ tsp turmeric
- ¼ tsp cayenne powder
- 4 large flour tortillas
- 1 cup cooked lentils
- ½ cup shredded cabbage
- ¼ cup minced red onions

Directions:

1. Preheat air fryer to 200°C/390°F.
2. Place the mashed potatoes, sunflower oil, garlic, lime, cumin, onion powder, coriander, salt, turmeric, and cayenne in a large bowl. Stir well until combined.
3. Lay the tortillas out flat on the counter. In the middle of each, distribute the potato filling. Add some of the lentils, cabbage, and red onions on top of the potatoes.
4. Close the wraps by folding the bottom of the tortillas up and over the filling, then folding the sides in, then roll the bottom up to form a burrito.
5. Place the wraps in the greased air fryer basket, seam side down. Air Fry for 6-8 minutes, flipping once until golden and crispy.
6. Serve topped with cilantro chutney.

Variations & Ingredients Tips:

- Make your own cilantro chutney by blending fresh cilantro, mint, green chili, lime juice, and salt.
- Use kidney beans or black beans instead of lentils for variation.
- Add shredded cheese to the filling for extra richness and flavor.

Per Serving: Calories: 510; Total Fat: 13g; Saturated Fat: 2g; Sodium: 820mg; Total Carbohydrates: 87g; Dietary Fiber: 13g; Total Sugars: 6g; Protein: 18g

Zucchini Tamale Pie

Servings: 4 | Prep Time: 15 Minutes | Cooking Time: 45 Minutes

Ingredients:

- 1 cup canned diced tomatoes with juice
- 1 zucchini, diced
- 3 tbsp safflower oil
- 1 cup cooked pinto beans
- 3 garlic cloves, minced
- 1 tbsp corn masa flour
- 1 tsp dried oregano
- 1/2 tsp ground cumin
- 1 tsp onion powder
- Salt to taste
- 1/2 tsp red chili flakes
- 1/2 cup ground cornmeal
- 1 tsp nutritional yeast
- 2 tbsp chopped cilantro
- 1/2 tsp lime zest

Directions:

1. Warm 2 tbsp of the oil in a skillet over medium heat and sauté the zucchini for 3 minutes or until they begin to brown.
2. Add the beans, tomatoes, garlic, flour, oregano, cumin, onion powder, salt, and chili flakes. Cook for 5 minutes until thick.

3. Remove from heat. Spray a baking pan with oil and pour the mix inside. Smooth the top and set aside.
4. In a pot, add the cornmeal, 1 1/2 cups water, and salt. Whisk as it boils. Reduce heat to low.
5. Add the yeast and oil and cook for 10 minutes, stirring often, until thick.
6. Remove. Preheat air fryer to 165°C/325°F.
7. Add cilantro and lime zest into the cornmeal mix and combine.
8. Spread it over the filling to form a crust topping.
9. Put in the frying basket and Bake for 20 minutes until golden.
10. Let cool for 5-10 minutes, then cut and serve.

Variations & Ingredients Tips:

- Use gluten-free cornmeal or masa harina for crust.
- Add vegan cheese shreds to the filling.
- Top with avocado slices and salsa.

Per Serving: Calories: 328; Total Fat: 15g; Saturated Fat: 1g; Sodium: 290mg; Total Carbohydrates: 45g; Dietary Fiber: 9g; Total Sugars: 7g; Protein: 9g

Eggplant Parmesan

Servings: 4 | Prep Time: 20 Minutes | Cooking Time: 8 Minutes Per Batch

Ingredients:

- 1 medium eggplant, 15-20 cm long
- salt
- 1 large egg
- 1 tablespoon water
- ⅔ cup panko breadcrumbs
- ⅓ cup grated Parmesan cheese, plus more for serving
- 1 tablespoon Italian seasoning
- ¾ teaspoon oregano
- oil for misting or cooking spray
- 1 680-gram jar marinara sauce
- 225 grams spaghetti, cooked
- pepper

Directions:

1. Preheat air fryer to 200°C/390°F.
2. Leaving peel intact, cut eggplant into 8 round slices about 2-cm thick. Salt to taste.
3. Beat egg and water in a shallow dish.
4. In another shallow dish, combine panko, Parmesan, Italian seasoning, and oregano.
5. Dip eggplant slices in egg wash and then crumbs, pressing lightly to coat.
6. Mist slices with oil or cooking spray.
7. Place 4 eggplant slices in air fryer basket and cook for 8 minutes, until brown and crispy.
8. While eggplant is cooking, heat marinara sauce.
9. Repeat step 7 to cook remaining eggplant slices.
10. To serve, place cooked spaghetti on plates and top with marinara and eggplant slices. At the table, pass extra Parmesan cheese and freshly ground black pepper.

Variations & Ingredients Tips:

- Substitute eggplant with zucchini or portobello mushrooms for a different veggie option.
- Use gluten-free breadcrumbs and pasta for a gluten-free version.
- Serve with a side salad or garlic bread for a complete meal.

Per Serving: Calories: 420; Cholesterol: 55mg; Total Fat: 11g; Saturated Fat: 3g; Sodium: 1180mg; Total Carbohydrates: 68g; Dietary Fiber: 9g; Total Sugars: 16g; Protein: 16g

Chili Tofu & Quinoa Bowls

Servings: 2 | Prep Time: 20 Minutes | Cooking Time: 30 Minutes

Ingredients:

- 1 cup diced peeled sweet potatoes
- ¼ cup chopped mixed bell peppers
- 1/8 cup sprouted green lentils
- ½ onion, sliced
- 1 tsp avocado oil
- 1/8 cup chopped carrots
- 225 grams extra-firm tofu, cubed
- ½ tsp smoked paprika
- ½ tsp chili powder
- ¼ tsp salt
- 2 tsp lime zest
- 1 cup cooked quinoa
- 2 lime wedges

Directions:

1. Preheat air fryer at 175°C/350°F. Combine the onion, carrots, bell peppers, green lentils, sweet potato, and avocado oil in a bowl. In another bowl, mix the tofu, paprika, chili powder, and salt. Add veggie mixture to

the frying basket and Air Fry for 8 minutes. Stir in tofu mixture and cook for 8 more minutes. Combine lime zest and quinoa. Divide into 2 serving bowls. Top each with the tofu mixture and squeeze a lime wedge over. Serve warm.

Variations & Ingredients Tips:

- Use tempeh or seitan instead of tofu for a different plant-based protein.
- Add diced avocado, cherry tomatoes, or cilantro for extra toppings.
- Serve with hot sauce or vegan sour cream on the side.

Per Serving: Calories: 460; Cholesterol: 0mg; Total Fat: 18g; Saturated Fat: 2g; Sodium: 420mg; Total Carbohydrates: 59g; Dietary Fiber: 12g; Total Sugars: 11g; Protein: 22g

Rigatoni With Roasted Onions, Fennel, Spinach And Lemon Pepper Ricotta

Servings: 2 | Prep Time: 10 Minutes | Cooking Time: 13 Minutes

Ingredients:

- 1 red onion, rough chopped into large chunks
- 2 teaspoons olive oil, divided
- 1 bulb fennel, sliced 0.6-cm thick
- ¾ cup ricotta cheese
- 1½ teaspoons finely chopped lemon zest, plus more for garnish
- 1 teaspoon lemon juice
- salt and freshly ground black pepper
- 227 grams dried rigatoni pasta
- 3 cups baby spinach leaves

Directions:

1. Bring a large stockpot of salted water to a boil on the stovetop and Preheat the air fryer to 200°C/400°F.
2. While the water is coming to a boil, toss the chopped onion in 1 teaspoon of olive oil and transfer to the air fryer basket. Air-fry at 200°C/400°F for 5 minutes.
3. Toss the sliced fennel with 1 teaspoon of olive oil and add this to the air fryer basket with the onions. Continue to air-fry at 200°C/400°F for 8 minutes, shaking the basket a few times during the cooking process.
4. Combine the ricotta cheese, lemon zest and juice, ¼ teaspoon of salt and freshly ground black pepper in a bowl and stir until smooth.
5. Add the dried rigatoni to the boiling water and cook according to the package directions. When the pasta is cooked al dente, reserve one cup of the pasta water and drain the pasta into a colander.
6. Place the spinach in a serving bowl and immediately transfer the hot pasta to the bowl, wilting the spinach. Add the roasted onions and fennel and toss together. Add a little pasta water to the dish if it needs moistening. Then, dollop the lemon pepper ricotta cheese on top and nestle it into the hot pasta. Garnish with more lemon zest if desired.

Variations & Ingredients Tips:

- Substitute fennel with sliced zucchini or eggplant.
- Use goat cheese or feta instead of ricotta for a tangy flavor.
- Add cooked chicken or shrimp for a non-vegetarian version.

Per Serving: Calories: 610; Total Fat: 19g; Saturated Fat: 9g; Sodium: 470mg; Total Carbohydrates: 89g; Dietary Fiber: 7g; Total Sugars: 8g; Protein: 24g

Mushroom-rice Stuffed Bell Peppers

Servings: 4 | Prep Time: 20 Minutes | Cooking Time: 30 Minutes

Ingredients:

- 4 red bell peppers, tops sliced
- 1 ½ cups cooked rice
- ¼ cup chopped leeks
- ¼ cup sliced mushrooms
- ¾ cup tomato sauce
- Salt and pepper to taste
- ¾ cup shredded mozzarella
- 2 tbsp parsley, chopped

Directions:

1. Fill a large pot of water and heat on high until it boils. Remove seeds and membranes from the peppers. Carefully place peppers into the boiling water for 5 minutes. Remove and set aside to cool.
2. Mix together rice, leeks, mushrooms, tomato sauce, parsley, salt, and pepper in a large bowl. Stuff each pepper with the rice mixture. Top with mozzarella.
3. Preheat air fryer to 180°C/350°F. Arrange the peppers on the greased air fryer basket and Bake for 10 min-

utes. Serve.

Variations & Ingredients Tips:

- Use quinoa, couscous, or cauliflower rice instead of regular rice.
- Add ground veggie crumbles or lentils for more protein.
- Top with hot sauce or sriracha for a spicy touch.

Per Serving: Calories: 210; Total Fat: 6g; Saturated Fat: 3.5g; Sodium: 420mg; Total Carbohydrates: 29g; Dietary Fiber: 4g; Total Sugars: 8g; Protein: 11g

Sushi-style Deviled Eggs

Servings: 4 | Prep Time: 15 Minutes | Cooking Time: 20 Minutes

Ingredients:

- ¼ cup crabmeat, shells discarded
- 4 eggs
- 2 tbsp mayonnaise
- ½ tsp soy sauce
- ¼ avocado, diced
- ¼ tsp wasabi powder
- 2 tbsp diced cucumber
- 1 sheet nori, sliced
- 8 jarred pickled ginger slices
- 1 tsp toasted sesame seeds
- 2 spring onions, sliced

Directions:

1. Preheat air fryer to 130°C/260°F.
2. Place the eggs in muffin cups to avoid bumping around and cracking during the cooking process. Add silicone cups to the air fryer basket and Air Fry for 15 minutes.
3. Remove and plunge the eggs immediately into an ice bath to cool, about 5 minutes. Carefully peel and slice them in half lengthwise.
4. Spoon yolks into a separate medium bowl and arrange white halves on a large plate. Mash the yolks with a fork. Stir in mayonnaise, soy sauce, avocado, and wasabi powder until smooth. Mix in cucumber and spoon into white halves.
5. Scatter eggs with crabmeat, nori, pickled ginger, spring onions and sesame seeds to serve.

Variations & Ingredients Tips:

- Use smoked salmon or cooked shrimp instead of crabmeat.
- Add a drizzle of sriracha or hot sauce for extra heat.
- Garnish with furikake seasoning or bonito flakes.

Per Serving: Calories: 160; Total Fat: 12g; Saturated Fat: 3g; Sodium: 310mg; Total Carbohydrates: 4g; Dietary Fiber: 2g; Total Sugars: 1g; Protein: 10g

Effortless Mac `n´ Cheese

Servings: 4 | Prep Time: 10 Minutes | Cooking Time: 15 Minutes

Ingredients:

- 1 cup heavy cream
- 1 cup milk
- ½ cup mozzarella cheese
- 2 tsp grated Parmesan cheese
- 455 grams cooked elbow macaroni

Directions:

1. Preheat air fryer to 200°C/400°F. Whisk the heavy cream, milk, mozzarella cheese, and Parmesan cheese until smooth in a bowl. Stir in the macaroni and pour into a baking dish. Cover with foil and Bake in the air fryer for 6 minutes. Remove foil and Bake until cooked through and bubbly, 3-5 minutes. Serve warm.

Variations & Ingredients Tips:

- Add diced jalapeños, bacon bits, or breadcrumbs for extra flavor and texture.
- Substitute elbow macaroni with penne, fusilli, or shells for a different pasta shape.
- Use a combination of different cheeses like cheddar, gouda, or Gruyère for a more complex flavor.

Per Serving: Calories: 640; Cholesterol: 125mg; Total Fat: 41g; Saturated Fat: 25g; Sodium: 360mg; Total Carbohydrates: 46g; Dietary Fiber: 2g; Total Sugars: 7g; Protein: 22g

Mushroom Lasagna

Servings: 4 | Prep Time: 20 Minutes | Cooking Time: 40 Minutes

Ingredients:

- 2 tbsp olive oil
- 1 zucchini, diced
- ½ cup diced mushrooms
- ¼ cup diced onion

- 1 cup marinara sauce
- 1 cup ricotta cheese
- 1/3 cup grated Parmesan
- 1 egg
- 2 tsp Italian seasoning
- 2 tbsp fresh basil, chopped
- ½ tsp thyme
- 1 tbsp red pepper flakes
- ½ tsp salt
- 5 lasagna noodle sheets
- 1 cup grated mozzarella

Directions:

1. Heat the oil in a skillet over medium heat. Add zucchini, mushrooms, 1 tbsp of basil, thyme, red pepper flakes and onion and cook for 4 minutes until the veggies are tender. Toss in marinara sauce, and bring it to a bowl. Then, low the heat and simmer for 3 minutes.
2. Preheat air fryer at 190°C/375°F.
3. Combine ricotta cheese, Parmesan cheese, egg, Italian seasoning, and salt in a bowl.
4. Spoon ¼ of the veggie mixture into a 20-cm cake pan. Add a layer of lasagna noodles on top, breaking apart noodles first to fit pan. Then, top with 1/3 of ricotta mixture and ¼ of mozzarella cheese. Repeat the layer 2 more times, finishing with mozzarella cheese on top. Cover cake pan with aluminum foil.
5. Place cake pan in the air fryer basket and Bake for 12 minutes. Remove the foil and cook for 3 more minutes.
6. Let rest for 10 minutes before slicing. Serve immediately sprinkled with the remaining fresh basil.

Variations & Ingredients Tips:

- Use eggplant or bell peppers instead of zucchini for a different veggie combination.
- Substitute marinara with Alfredo sauce for a white lasagna version.
- Add a layer of cooked spinach or kale for extra nutrients and color.

Per Serving: Calories: 460; Total Fat: 27g; Saturated Fat: 13g; Sodium: 1020mg; Total Carbohydrates: 32g; Dietary Fiber: 3g; Total Sugars: 7g; Protein: 26g

Spicy Sesame Tempeh Slaw With Peanut Dressing

Servings: 2 | Prep Time: 20 Minutes (plus Marinating Time) | Cooking Time: 8 Minutes

Ingredients:

- 2 cups hot water
- 1 teaspoon salt
- 227 grams tempeh, sliced into 2.5-cm-long pieces
- 2 tablespoons low-sodium soy sauce
- 2 tablespoons rice vinegar
- 1 tablespoon filtered water
- 2 teaspoons sesame oil
- ½ teaspoon fresh ginger
- 1 clove garlic, minced
- ¼ teaspoon black pepper
- ½ jalapeño, sliced
- 4 cups cabbage slaw
- 4 tablespoons Peanut Dressing (see the following recipe)
- 2 tablespoons fresh chopped cilantro
- 2 tablespoons chopped peanuts

Directions:

1. Mix the hot water with the salt and pour over the tempeh in a glass bowl. Stir and cover with a towel for 10 minutes.
2. Discard the water and leave the tempeh in the bowl.
3. In a medium bowl, mix the soy sauce, rice vinegar, filtered water, sesame oil, ginger, garlic, pepper, and jalapeño. Pour over the tempeh and cover with a towel. Place in the refrigerator to marinate for at least 2 hours.
4. Preheat the air fryer to 190°C/370°F. Remove the tempeh from the bowl and discard the remaining marinade.
5. Liberally spray the metal trivet that goes into the air fryer basket and place the tempeh on top of the trivet.
6. Cook for 4 minutes, flip, and cook another 4 minutes.
7. In a large bowl, mix the cabbage slaw with the Peanut Dressing and toss in the cilantro and chopped peanuts.
8. Portion onto 4 plates and place the cooked tempeh on top when cooking completes. Serve immediately.

Variations & Ingredients Tips:

- Use extra-firm tofu instead of tempeh for a different protein.
- Add shredded carrots, bell peppers, or edamame to the slaw.
- Substitute peanut dressing with a sesame-ginger dressing.

Per Serving: Calories: 380; Total Fat: 23g; Saturated Fat: 3.5g; Sodium: 1210mg; Total Carbohydrates: 29g; Dietary Fiber: 8g; Total Sugars: 8g; Protein: 22g

Chive Potato Pierogi

Servings: 4 | Prep Time: 25 Minutes | Cooking Time: 55 Minutes

Ingredients:

- 2 boiled potatoes (around 340g), mashed
- Salt and pepper to taste
- 1 tsp cumin powder
- 2 tbsp sour cream
- 1/4 cup grated Parmesan
- 2 tbsp chopped chives
- 1 tbsp chopped parsley
- 1 1/4 cups flour
- 1/4 tsp garlic powder
- 3/4 cup Greek yogurt
- 1 egg
- Cooking spray or oil for greasing

Directions:

1. Combine the mashed potatoes along with sour cream, cumin, parsley, chives, pepper, and salt and stir until slightly chunky.
2. Mix the flour, salt, and garlic powder in a large bowl. Stir in yogurt until it comes together as a sticky dough. Knead in the bowl for about 2-3 minutes to make it smooth.
3. Whisk the egg and 1 teaspoon of water in a small bowl.
4. Roll out the dough on a lightly floured work surface to 6-mm thickness. Cut out 12 circles with a cookie cutter.
5. Preheat air fryer to 175°C/350°F.
6. Divide the potato mixture and Parmesan cheese between the dough circles. Brush the edges with the egg wash and fold the dough over the filling into half-moon shapes. Crimp the edges with a fork to seal.
7. Arrange the pierogies on the greased frying basket and Air Fry for 8-10 minutes, turning once, until the outside is golden.
8. Serve warm.

Variations & Ingredients Tips:

- Add cooked bacon or caramelized onions to the potato filling for extra flavor.
- Substitute Greek yogurt with sour cream or milk in the dough if desired.
- Serve with a side of sauteed mushrooms or roasted vegetables.

Per Serving (3 pierogies): Calories: 320, Total Fat: 9g, Saturated Fat: 4g, Cholesterol: 60mg, Sodium: 310mg, Total Carbs: 46g, Dietary Fiber: 3g, Total Sugars: 3g, Protein: 12g

Cheddar-bean Flautas

Servings: 4 | Prep Time: 10 Minutes | Cooking Time: 15 Minutes

Ingredients:

- 8 corn tortillas
- 1 can refried beans
- 1 cup shredded cheddar
- 1 cup guacamole

Directions:

1. Preheat air fryer to 200°C/390°F. Wet the tortillas with water. Spray the frying basket with oil and stack the tortillas inside. Air Fry for 1 minute. Remove to a flat surface, laying them out individually. Scoop an equal amount of beans in a line down the center of each tortilla. Top with cheddar cheese. Roll the tortilla sides over the filling and put seam-side down in the greased frying basket. Air Fry for 7 minutes or until the tortillas are golden and crispy. Serve immediately topped with guacamole.

Variations & Ingredients Tips:

- Use black beans or pinto beans instead of refried beans for a different flavor.
- Add diced onions, jalapeños, or cilantro to the bean mixture for extra kick.
- Serve with salsa, sour cream, or hot sauce on the side.

Per Serving (2 flautas): Calories: 430; Cholesterol: 25mg; Total Fat: 23g; Saturated Fat: 9g; Sodium: 850mg; Total Carbohydrates: 46g; Dietary Fiber: 9g; Total Sugars: 2g; Protein: 16g

Easy Zucchini Lasagna Roll-ups

Servings: 2 | Prep Time: 20 Minutes | Cooking Time: 40 Minutes

Ingredients:

- 2 medium zucchini
- 2 tbsp lemon juice
- 1 ½ cups ricotta cheese
- 1 tbsp allspice
- 2 cups marinara sauce

- 1/3 cup mozzarella cheese

Directions:

1. Preheat air fryer to 200°C/400°F. Cut the ends of each zucchini, then slice into 6-mm thick pieces and drizzle with lemon juice. Roast for 5 minutes until slightly tender. Let cool slightly. Combine ricotta cheese and allspice in a bowl; set aside. Spread 2 tbsp of marinara sauce on the bottom of a baking pan. Spoon 1-2 tbsp of the ricotta mixture onto each slice, roll up each slice and place them spiral-side up in the pan. Scatter with the remaining ricotta mixture and drizzle with marinara sauce. Top with mozzarella cheese and Bake at 180°C/360°F for 20 minutes until the cheese is bubbly and golden brown. Serve warm.

Variations & Ingredients Tips:

- Substitute zucchini with eggplant or lasagna noodles for different textures.
- Add minced garlic, basil, or oregano to the ricotta mixture for extra flavor.
- Top with grated Parmesan cheese or breadcrumbs before baking for a crispy crust.

Per Serving: Calories: 470; Cholesterol: 80mg; Total Fat: 25g; Saturated Fat: 15g; Sodium: 1060mg; Total Carbohydrates: 38g; Dietary Fiber: 7g; Total Sugars: 22g; Protein: 29g

Vegetarian Stuffed Bell Peppers

Servings: 3 | Prep Time: 15 Minutes | Cooking Time: 40 Minutes

Ingredients:

- 1 cup mushrooms, chopped
- 1 tbsp allspice
- 3/4 cup Alfredo sauce
- 1/2 cup canned diced tomatoes
- 1 cup cooked rice
- 2 tbsp dried parsley
- 2 tbsp hot sauce
- Salt and pepper to taste
- 3 large bell peppers

Directions:

1. Preheat air fryer to 190°C/375°F.
2. Whisk mushrooms, allspice and 1 cup of boiling water until smooth.
3. Stir in Alfredo sauce, tomatoes and juices, rice, parsley, hot sauce, salt, and black pepper. Set aside.
4. Cut the top of each bell pepper, take out the core and seeds without breaking the pepper.
5. Fill each pepper with the rice mixture and cover them with a 15-cm square of aluminum foil, folding the edges.
6. Roast for 30 minutes until tender.
7. Let cool completely before unwrapping. Serve immediately.

Variations & Ingredients Tips:

- Use different grains like quinoa or farro instead of rice.
- Add vegan cheese shreds to the filling.
- Top with vegan sour cream or cashew cream.

Per Serving: Calories: 316; Total Fat: 14g; Saturated Fat: 3g; Sodium: 1156mg; Total Carbohydrates: 42g; Dietary Fiber: 5g; Total Sugars: 10g; Protein: 8g

Mexican Twice Air-fried Sweet Potatoes

Servings: 2 | Prep Time: 15 Minutes | Cooking Time: 42 Minutes

Ingredients:

- 2 large sweet potatoes
- Olive oil
- Salt and freshly ground black pepper
- 1/3 cup diced red onion
- 1/3 cup diced red bell pepper
- 1/2 cup canned black beans, drained and rinsed
- 1/2 cup corn kernels, fresh or frozen
- 1/2 teaspoon chili powder
- 1 1/2 cups grated pepper jack cheese, divided
- Jalapeño peppers, sliced

Directions:

1. Preheat the air fryer to 200°C/400°F.
2. Rub the sweet potatoes with olive oil and season with salt and pepper. Air fry at 400°F for 30 minutes, rotating occasionally.
3. Make the filling: Sauté onion and pepper. Add black beans, corn, and chili powder and sauté for 3 minutes. Set aside.
4. Remove potatoes, let rest 5 minutes. Slice off one cm of the flattest sides.
5. Scoop out potato flesh into a bowl, leaving 1.3-cm

around edges.
6. Mash potato flesh. Add filling and 1 cup cheese. Season and mix well.
7. Stuff potato shells with filling, mounding high.
8. Air fry stuffed potatoes at 190°C/370°F for 10 minutes.
9. Top with remaining cheese, lower heat to 170°C/340°F and cook 2 more minutes to melt cheese.
10. Top with jalapeños and serve warm.

Variations & Ingredients Tips:

- Use vegan cheese shreds for a dairy-free option.
- Add diced avocado or pico de gallo as toppers.
- Swap black beans for pinto or kidney beans.

Per Serving: Calories: 653; Total Fat: 27g; Saturated Fat: 14g; Sodium: 877mg; Total Carbohydrates: 82g; Dietary Fiber: 16g; Total Sugars: 15g; Protein: 25g

Mushroom, Zucchini And Black Bean Burgers

Servings: 4 | Prep Time: 20 Minutes | Cooking Time: 18 Minutes

Ingredients:

- 1 cup diced zucchini (about 1/2 medium zucchini)
- 1 tablespoon olive oil
- Salt and freshly ground black pepper
- 1 cup chopped brown mushrooms (about 85 g)
- 1 small clove garlic
- 1 (425 g) can black beans, drained and rinsed
- 1 teaspoon lemon zest
- 1 tablespoon chopped fresh cilantro
- 1/2 cup plain breadcrumbs
- 1 egg, beaten
- 1/2 teaspoon salt
- Freshly ground black pepper
- Whole-wheat pita bread, burger buns or brioche buns
- Mayonnaise, tomato, avocado and lettuce, for serving

Directions:

1. Preheat the air fryer to 200°C/400°F.
2. Toss the zucchini with olive oil, season with salt and pepper and air fry for 6 minutes, shaking once or twice.
3. Transfer zucchini to a food processor with mushrooms, garlic and black beans. Process until chunky and pasty.
4. Transfer mixture to a bowl. Add zest, cilantro, breadcrumbs, egg, salt and pepper. Mix well.
5. Shape into 4 patties and refrigerate for 15 minutes.
6. Preheat air fryer to 190°C/370°F.
7. Air fry 2 patties for 12 minutes, flipping halfway. Keep warm.
8. Cook remaining 2 patties same way. Return first batch for last 2 mins to reheat.
9. Serve on buns with desired toppings.

Variations & Ingredients Tips:

- Use gluten-free bread crumbs or oats for binding.
- Add diced bell peppers or shredded carrots to the patty mix.
- Top with guacamole, salsa or vegan cheese slices.

Per Serving: Calories: 290; Total Fat: 9g; Saturated Fat: 1g; Sodium: 670mg; Total Carbohydrates: 42g; Dietary Fiber: 12g; Total Sugars: 3g; Protein: 14g

Powerful Jackfruit Fritters

Servings: 4 | Prep Time: 20 Minutes | Cooking Time: 30 Minutes

Ingredients:

- 1 can jackfruit, chopped
- 1 egg, beaten
- 1 tbsp Dijon mustard
- 1 tbsp mayonnaise
- 1 tbsp prepared horseradish
- 2 tbsp grated yellow onion
- 2 tbsp chopped parsley
- 2 tbsp chopped nori
- 2 tbsp flour
- 1 tbsp Cajun seasoning
- ¼ tsp garlic powder
- ¼ tsp salt
- 2 lemon wedges

Directions:

1. In a bowl, combine jackfruit, egg, mustard, mayonnaise, horseradish, onion, parsley, nori, flour, Cajun seasoning, garlic, and salt. Let chill in the fridge for 15 minutes.
2. Preheat air fryer to 180°C/350°F.
3. Divide the mixture into 12 balls. Place them in the air fryer basket and Air Fry for 10 minutes.
4. Serve with lemon wedges.

Variations & Ingredients Tips:

- Substitute jackfruit with canned artichoke hearts or hearts of palm.
- Use Old Bay seasoning instead of Cajun for a different spice profile.
- Serve with tartar sauce or spicy remoulade.

Per Serving: Calories: 120; Total Fat: 5g; Saturated Fat: 1g; Sodium: 730mg; Total Carbohydrates: 16g; Dietary Fiber: 3g; Total Sugars: 6g; Protein: 4g

Italian-style Fried Cauliflower

Servings: 4 | Prep Time: 25 Minutes | Cooking Time: 35 Minutes

Ingredients:

- 2 eggs
- 1/3 cup all-purpose flour
- ½ tsp Italian seasoning
- ½ cup bread crumbs
- 1 tsp garlic powder
- 3 tsp grated Parmesan cheese
- Salt and pepper to taste
- 1 head cauliflower, cut into florets
- ½ tsp ground coriander

Directions:

1. Preheat air fryer to 190°C/370°F.
2. Set out 3 small bowls. In the first, mix the flour with Italian seasoning. In the second, beat the eggs. In the third bowl, combine the crumbs, garlic, Parmesan, ground coriander, salt, and pepper.
3. Dip the cauliflower in the flour, then dredge in egg, and finally in the bread crumb mixture.
4. Place a batch of cauliflower in the greased air fryer basket and spray with cooking oil.
5. Bake for 10-12 minutes, shaking once until golden.
6. Serve warm and enjoy!

Variations & Ingredients Tips:

- Use panko breadcrumbs for an extra crispy texture.
- Add red pepper flakes or cayenne to the breading for a spicy kick.
- Serve with marinara sauce or ranch dressing for dipping.

Per Serving: Calories: 170; Total Fat: 5g; Saturated Fat: 1.5g; Sodium: 410mg; Total Carbohydrates: 24g; Dietary Fiber: 5g; Total Sugars: 4g; Protein: 9g

Party Giant Nachos

Servings: 2 | Prep Time: 10 Minutes | Cooking Time: 20 Minutes

Ingredients:

- 2 tbsp sour cream
- ½ tsp chili powder
- Salt to taste
- 2 soft corn tortillas
- 2 tsp avocado oil
- ½ cup refried beans
- ¼ cup cheddar cheese shreds
- 2 tbsp Parmesan cheese
- 2 tbsp sliced black olives
- ¼ cup torn iceberg lettuce
- ¼ cup baby spinach
- ½ sliced avocado
- 1 tomato, diced
- 2 lime wedges

Directions:

1. Preheat air fryer at 200°C/400°F.
2. Whisk the sour cream, chili powder, and salt in a small bowl.
3. Brush tortillas with avocado oil and season one side with salt. Place tortillas in the air fryer basket and Bake for 3 minutes. Set aside.
4. Layer the refried beans, Parmesan and cheddar cheeses in the tortillas. Place them back into the basket and Bake for 2 minutes.
5. Divide tortillas into 2 serving plates. Top each tortilla with black olives, baby spinach, lettuce, and tomatoes. Dollop sour cream mixture on each.
6. Serve with lime and avocado wedges on the side.

Variations & Ingredients Tips:

- Add sliced jalapeños or hot sauce for a spicy kick.
- Use Greek yogurt instead of sour cream for a healthier option.
- Substitute refried beans with black beans or pinto beans.

Per Serving: Calories: 380; Total Fat: 24g; Saturated Fat: 7g; Sodium: 780mg; Total Carbohydrates: 32g; Dietary Fiber: 9g; Total Sugars: 5g; Protein: 13g

Vegetable Side Dishes Recipes

Garlic-parmesan Popcorn

Servings: 2 | Prep Time: 2 Minutes | Cooking Time: 15 Minutes

Ingredients:

- 2 tsp grated Parmesan cheese
- ¼ cup popcorn kernels
- 1 tbsp lemon juice
- 1 tsp garlic powder

Directions:

1. Preheat air fryer to 200°C/400°F. Line basket with foil.
2. Put kernels in a single layer and Grill for 6-8 minutes until popping stops.
3. Remove popped corn to a bowl.
4. Drizzle with lemon juice and toss to coat.
5. Sprinkle with garlic powder and parmesan and toss again.
6. Drizzle with more lemon juice.
7. Serve.

Variations & Ingredients Tips:

- Use olive oil or melted butter instead of lemon juice.
- Add red pepper flakes or paprika for spice.
- Substitute nutritional yeast for a dairy-free "cheesy" flavor.

Per Serving: Calories: 90; Total Fat: 1g; Saturated Fat: 0g; Cholesterol: 0mg; Sodium: 90mg; Total Carbs: 16g; Fiber: 2g; Sugars: 0g; Protein: 3g

Healthy Caprese Salad

Servings: 2 | Prep Time: 5 Minutes | Cooking Time: 20 Minutes

Ingredients:

- 1 (125g) ball mozzarella cheese, sliced
- 16 grape tomatoes
- 2 tsp olive oil
- Salt and pepper to taste
- 1 tbsp balsamic vinegar
- 1 tsp mixed seeds
- 1 tbsp chopped basil

Directions:

1. Preheat air fryer at 180°C/350°F.
2. Toss tomatoes with 1 tsp of olive oil and salt in a bowl.
3. Place them in the frying basket and air fry for 15 minutes, shaking twice.
4. Divide mozzarella slices between 2 serving plates, top with blistered tomatoes.
5. Drizzle with balsamic vinegar and the remaining olive oil.
6. Sprinkle with basil, black pepper and the mixed seeds and serve.

Variations & Ingredients Tips:

- Add sliced avocado or grilled chicken for extra protein.
- Use balsamic glaze instead of vinegar for a thicker dressing.
- Top with pesto instead of basil.

Per Serving: Calories: 215; Total Fat: 15g; Saturated Fat: 6g; Cholesterol: 30mg; Sodium: 290mg; Total Carbs: 8g; Dietary Fiber: 2g; Total Sugars: 5g; Protein: 13g

Asparagus

Servings: 4 | Prep Time: 5 Minutes | Cooking Time: 9 Minutes

Ingredients:

- 1 bunch asparagus (approx. 454g), washed and trimmed
- ⅛ teaspoon dried tarragon, crushed
- Salt and pepper
- 1 to 2 teaspoons extra-light olive oil

Directions:

1. Spread asparagus spears on cookie sheet or cutting board.
2. Sprinkle with tarragon, salt, and pepper.

3. Drizzle with 1 teaspoon of oil and roll the spears or mix by hand. If needed, add up to 1 more teaspoon of oil and mix again until all spears are lightly coated.
4. Place spears in air fryer basket. If necessary, bend the longer spears to make them fit. It doesn't matter if they don't lie flat.
5. Cook at 200°C/390°F for 5 minutes. Shake basket or stir spears with a spoon.
6. Cook for an additional 4 minutes or just until crisp-tender.

Variations & Ingredients Tips:

- Toss with lemon zest and parmesan before cooking.
- Add a drizzle of balsamic glaze after cooking.
- Sprinkle with crushed red pepper flakes for a kick of heat.

Per Serving: Calories: 40; Total Fat: 2g; Saturated Fat: 0g; Cholesterol: 0mg; Sodium: 5mg; Total Carbs: 4g; Fiber: 2g; Sugars: 2g; Protein: 3g

Thyme Sweet Potato Wedges

Servings: 4 | Prep Time: 10 Minutes | Cooking Time: 30 Minutes

Ingredients:

- 2 peeled sweet potatoes, cubed
- 30 g grated Parmesan
- 1 tablespoon olive oil
- Salt and pepper to taste
- ½ teaspoon dried thyme
- ½ teaspoon ground cumin

Directions:

1. Preheat air fryer to 165°C/330°F.
2. Add sweet potato cubes to the frying basket, then drizzle with oil. Toss to gently coat.
3. Season with salt, pepper, thyme, and cumin.
4. Roast the potatoes for about 10 minutes. Shake the basket and continue roasting for another 10 minutes.
5. Shake the basket again, this time adding Parmesan cheese. Shake and return to the air fryer.
6. Roast until the potatoes are tender, 4-6 minutes.
7. Serve and enjoy!

Variations & Ingredients Tips:

- Use different types of potatoes, such as russet or Yukon Gold, for a variety of flavors and textures.
- Add some minced garlic or red pepper flakes for extra flavor.
- Serve the sweet potato wedges with a dipping sauce, such as ranch dressing or garlic aioli.

Per Serving: Calories: 140; Total Fat: 5g; Saturated Fat: 1.5g; Cholesterol: 5mg; Sodium: 180mg; Total Carbs: 21g; Fiber: 3g; Sugars: 5g; Protein: 4g

Cauliflower

Servings: 4 | Prep Time: 2 Minutes | Cooking Time: 6 Minutes

Ingredients:

- ½ cup water
- 1 283g package frozen cauliflower (florets)
- 1 teaspoon lemon pepper seasoning

Directions:

1. Pour the water into air fryer drawer.
2. Pour the frozen cauliflower into the air fryer basket and sprinkle with lemon pepper seasoning.
3. Cook at 198°C/390°F for approximately 6 minutes.

Variations & Ingredients Tips:

- Toss with olive oil, garlic and parmesan before air frying.
- Add smoked paprika or curry powder for extra flavor.
- Serve with lemon wedges for squeezing over top.

Per Serving: Calories: 25; Total Fat: 0g; Saturated Fat: 0g; Cholesterol: 0mg; Sodium: 20mg; Total Carbs: 5g; Fiber: 2g; Sugars: 2g; Protein: 2g

Crispy, Cheesy Leeks

Servings: 4 | Prep Time: 10 Minutes | Cooking Time: 15 Minutes

Ingredients:

- 2 Medium leeks, about 255g each
- Olive oil spray
- ¼ cup Seasoned Italian-style dried bread crumbs (gluten-free, if a concern)
- ¼ cup (about 21g) Finely grated Parmesan cheese
- 2 tablespoons Olive oil

Directions:

1. Preheat air fryer to 177°C/350°F.
2. Trim leek ends, halve lengthwise. Remove inner layer halfway down. Coat all sides with olive oil spray.
3. Place leeks cut-side up in basket with space between pieces. Air fry 12 mins.
4. Meanwhile, mix breadcrumbs, cheese, and olive oil.
5. After 12 mins, sprinkle breadcrumb mixture over leeks. Increase to 190-198°C/375-390°F. Air fry 3 more mins until topping browns.
6. Transfer leeks to platter. Cool briefly before serving.

Variations & Ingredients Tips:

- Add lemon zest and parsley to the breadcrumb mixture.
- Use panko breadcrumbs for extra crunch.
- Drizzle with balsamic glaze before serving.

Per Serving: Calories: 130; Total Fat: 9g; Saturated Fat: 2g; Cholesterol: 5mg; Sodium: 160mg; Total Carbs: 10g; Fiber: 2g; Sugars: 2g; Protein: 3g

Blistered Green Beans

Servings: 3 | Prep Time: 5 Minutes | Cooking Time: 10 Minutes

Ingredients:

- 340g Green beans, trimmed on both ends
- 1½ tablespoons Olive oil
- 3 tablespoons Pine nuts
- 1½ tablespoons Balsamic vinegar
- 1½ teaspoons Minced garlic
- ¾ teaspoon Table salt
- ¾ teaspoon Ground black pepper

Directions:

1. Preheat the air fryer to 200°C/400°F.
2. Toss the green beans and oil in a large bowl until all the green beans are glistening.
3. When the machine is at temperature, pile the green beans into the basket. Air-fry for 10 minutes, tossing often to rearrange the green beans in the basket, or until blistered and tender.
4. Dump the contents of the basket into a serving bowl. Add the pine nuts, vinegar, garlic, salt, and pepper. Toss well to coat and combine. Serve warm or at room temperature.

Variations & Ingredients Tips:

- Add crushed red pepper flakes for a kick of heat.
- Substitute walnuts or sliced almonds for the pine nuts.
- Toss with grated parmesan before serving.

Per Serving: Calories: 150; Total Fat: 11g; Saturated Fat: 1g; Cholesterol: 0mg; Sodium: 460mg; Total Carbs: 10g; Fiber: 4g; Sugars: 4g; Protein: 4g

Cheesy Texas Toast

Servings: 2 | Prep Time: 5 Minutes | Cooking Time: 4 Minutes

Ingredients:

- 2 2.5cm-thick slices Italian bread (each about 10cm across)
- 4 teaspoons Softened butter
- 2 teaspoons Minced garlic
- ¼ cup (about 21g) Finely grated Parmesan cheese

Directions:

1. Preheat the air fryer to 200°C/400°F.
2. Spread one side of each bread slice with 2 tsp butter. Sprinkle with 1 tsp minced garlic, followed by 2 tbsp grated cheese.
3. When the machine is at temperature, put the bread slices cheese side up in the basket with space between them.
4. Air-fry undisturbed for 4 minutes, or until browned and crunchy.
5. Use a nonstick-safe spatula to transfer the toasts cheese side up to a wire rack. Cool for 5 minutes before serving.

Variations & Ingredients Tips:

- Add dried Italian seasoning or crushed red pepper to the butter.
- Use different cheese varieties like cheddar, provolone or asiago.
- Brush with garlic butter instead of plain butter.

Per Serving: Calories: 320; Total Fat: 18g; Saturated Fat: 9g; Cholesterol: 35mg; Sodium: 820mg; Total Carbs: 30g; Fiber: 1g; Sugars: 1g; Protein: 10g

Fried Green Tomatoes With Sriracha Mayo

Servings: 4 | Prep Time: 15 Minutes | Cooking

Time: 12 Minutes

Ingredients:

- 3 green tomatoes
- Salt and freshly ground black pepper
- ⅓ cup all-purpose flour
- 2 eggs
- ½ cup buttermilk
- 1 cup panko breadcrumbs
- 1 cup cornmeal
- Olive oil spray
- Fresh thyme sprigs or chopped chives
- Sriracha Mayo:
- ½ cup mayonnaise
- 1-2 tablespoons sriracha hot sauce
- 1 tablespoon milk

Directions:

1. Cut tomatoes into 6mm slices. Pat dry and season with salt and pepper.
2. Set up 3 dishes: 1 with flour, 1 with eggs+buttermilk, 1 with panko+cornmeal.
3. Preheat air fryer to 200°C/400°F.
4. Dredge tomatoes in flour, egg wash, then breadcrumb mixture to coat.
5. Spray basket with oil. Air fry 3-4 tomato slices for 8 mins. Flip and fry 4 more mins until golden.
6. Make sriracha mayo by mixing ingredients.
7. Stack fried tomatoes in basket, air fry 1-2 mins to reheat before serving.
8. Serve hot with sriracha mayo, salt, pepper and thyme/chives.

Variations & Ingredients Tips:

- Use yellow cornmeal for a crunchier coating.
- Add cajun seasoning or hot sauce to the egg wash.
- Substitute Greek yogurt for some of the mayo.

Per Serving: Calories: 390; Total Fat: 18g; Saturated Fat: 3g; Cholesterol: 105mg; Sodium: 400mg; Total Carbs: 48g; Fiber: 4g; Sugars: 5g; Protein: 9g

Perfect Broccoli

Servings: 4 | Prep Time: 5 Minutes | Cooking Time: 12 Minutes

Ingredients:

- 5 cups (624g) fresh broccoli florets
- Olive oil spray
- 3/4 teaspoon table salt

Directions:

1. Preheat air fryer to 190°C/375°F.
2. Place broccoli florets in a bowl and coat generously with olive oil spray, tossing to evenly coat.
3. Sprinkle with salt and toss again.
4. Pour florets into air fryer basket in an even layer.
5. Air fry for 10 minutes, tossing and rearranging pieces twice during cooking until lightly browned but still crunchy.
6. Transfer florets to a serving bowl and let cool 1-2 minutes before serving hot.

Variations & Ingredients Tips:

- Add minced garlic or red pepper flakes before cooking.
- Toss with lemon juice, parmesan or breadcrumbs after cooking.
- Use frozen broccoli florets and increase cook time by 2-3 minutes.

Per Serving: Calories: 33; Total Fat: 1g; Saturated Fat: 0g; Cholesterol: 0mg; Sodium: 298mg; Total Carbohydrates: 5g; Dietary Fiber: 3g; Total Sugars: 2g; Protein: 3g

Dijon Artichoke Hearts

Servings: 4 | Prep Time: 10 Minutes | Cooking Time: 25 Minutes

Ingredients:

- 1 jar artichoke hearts in water, drained
- 1 egg
- 1 tbsp Dijon mustard
- ½ cup bread crumbs
- ¼ cup flour
- 6 basil leaves

Directions:

1. Preheat air fryer to 177°C/350°F.
2. Beat egg and mustard in a bowl.
3. In another bowl, combine bread crumbs and flour.
4. Dip artichoke hearts in egg mixture, then dredge in crumb mixture.
5. Place artichoke hearts in the greased frying basket and Air Fry for 7-10 minutes until crispy.
6. Serve topped with basil.

Variations & Ingredients Tips:

▶ Use panko breadcrumbs for extra crunch.
▶ Add parmesan cheese to the breadcrumb mixture.
▶ Serve with a lemon garlic aioli for dipping.

Per Serving: Calories: 180; Total Fat: 5g; Saturated Fat: 1g; Cholesterol: 55mg; Sodium: 420mg; Total Carbs: 29g; Fiber: 6g; Sugars: 2g; Protein: 7g

Fried Cauliflower With Parmesan Lemon Dressing

Servings: 2 | Prep Time: 5 Minutes | Cooking Time: 12 Minutes

Ingredients:

- 4 cups cauliflower florets (about 340g)
- 1 tablespoon olive oil
- Salt and freshly ground black pepper
- 1 teaspoon finely chopped lemon zest
- 1 tablespoon fresh lemon juice
- ¼ cup grated Parmigiano-Reggiano cheese
- 4 tablespoons extra virgin olive oil
- ¼ teaspoon salt
- Freshly ground black pepper
- 1 tablespoon chopped fresh parsley

Directions:

1. Preheat air fryer to 200°C/400°F.
2. Toss cauliflower with 1 tbsp olive oil, salt and pepper.
3. Air fry for 12 mins, shaking basket a few times.
4. Make dressing: Combine lemon zest, juice, parmesan, 4 tbsp olive oil, ¼ tsp salt, pepper.
5. Toss fried cauliflower with dressing and parsley.

Variations & Ingredients Tips:

▶ Use a gluten-free coating instead of olive oil.
▶ Add crushed red pepper flakes or garlic to the dressing.
▶ Sprinkle with toasted panko breadcrumbs before serving.

Per Serving: Calories: 320; Total Fat: 30g; Saturated Fat: 5g; Cholesterol: 10mg; Sodium: 420mg; Total Carbs: 10g; Fiber: 4g; Sugars: 4g; Protein: 6g

Crispy Cauliflower Puffs

Servings: 12 Puffs | Prep Time: 10 Minutes | Cooking Time: 9 Minutes

Ingredients:

- 1½ cups Riced cauliflower
- 1 cup (about 113g) Shredded Monterey Jack cheese
- ¾ cup Seasoned Italian-style panko bread crumbs (gluten-free, if a concern)
- 2 tablespoons plus 1 teaspoon All-purpose flour or potato starch
- 2 tablespoons plus 1 teaspoon Vegetable oil
- 1 plus 1 large egg yolk
- ¾ teaspoon Table salt
- Vegetable oil spray

Directions:

1. Preheat the air fryer to 190°C/375°F.
2. Stir the riced cauliflower, cheese, bread crumbs, flour or potato starch, oil, eggs and salt in a bowl to make a thick batter.
3. Using 2 tbsp of the batter, form compact balls between your palms. Make 7 more for a small batch, 11 more for medium, or 15 more for large.
4. Generously coat the balls with vegetable oil spray. Set them in the basket with space between them.
5. Air-fry undisturbed for 7 mins, or until golden brown and crisp. If 182°C/360°F, may need 2 more mins.
6. Pour contents onto a wire rack. Cool puffs for 5 mins before serving.

Variations & Ingredients Tips:

▶ Add garlic powder, Italian seasoning or parmesan to the batter.
▶ Serve with marinara sauce for dipping.
▶ Use broccoli or cauliflower rice instead of riced cauliflower.
▶ Per Puff: Calories: 90; Total Fat: 6g; Saturated Fat: 2g; Cholesterol: 35mg; Sodium: 220mg; Total Carbs: 6g; Fiber: 1g; Sugars: 1g; Protein: 4g

Panko-crusted Zucchini Fries

Servings: 6 | Prep Time: 15 Minutes | Cooking Time: 8 Minutes

Ingredients:

- 3 medium zucchini
- 1/2 cup flour

- 1 teaspoon salt, divided
- 1/2 teaspoon black pepper, divided
- 3/4 teaspoon dried thyme, divided
- 2 large eggs
- 1 1/2 cups whole-wheat or plain panko breadcrumbs
- 1/2 cup grated Parmesan cheese

Directions:

1. Preheat the air fryer to 193°C/380°F.
2. Slice the zucchini into 1.25cm thick fry-like strips.
3. In a bowl, mix flour, 1/2 tsp salt, 1/4 tsp pepper, 1/2 tsp thyme.
4. In another bowl, whisk eggs, remaining 1/2 tsp salt, 1/4 tsp pepper.
5. In a third bowl, mix breadcrumbs, cheese, remaining 1/4 tsp thyme.
6. Dip zucchini in flour, then egg, then breadcrumb mixture to coat.
7. Arrange breaded fries in air fryer basket, spray with oil, and cook 4 mins.
8. Shake basket and cook 4-6 more mins until golden brown.
9. Serve warm.

Variations & Ingredients Tips:

▶ Add parmesan or ranch seasoning to the breadcrumb mixture.
▶ Use gluten-free breadcrumbs for a gluten-free version.
▶ Serve with marinara, ranch or cheese sauce for dipping.

Per Serving: Calories: 156; Total Fat: 5g; Saturated Fat: 2g; Cholesterol: 58mg; Sodium: 500mg; Total Carbohydrates: 22g; Dietary Fiber: 3g; Total Sugars: 3g; Protein: 8g

Salmon Salad With Steamboat Dressing

Servings: 4 | Prep Time: 20 Minutes | Cooking Time: 18 Minutes

Ingredients:

- 1/4 teaspoon salt
- 1 1/2 teaspoons dried dill
- 1 tablespoon fresh lemon juice
- 227g fresh or frozen salmon fillet, skin on
- 8 cups shredded romaine or leaf lettuce
- 8 asparagus spears, cooked and cut into 2.5cm pieces
- 8 cherry tomatoes, halved or quartered
- Steamboat dressing (not included in ingredients)

Directions:

1. Mix salt and dill. Rub lemon juice over salmon then sprinkle with dill-salt. Refrigerate 15-20 mins.
2. Make the steamboat dressing and refrigerate.
3. Cook salmon in air fryer at 165°C/330°F for 18 mins until flaky but moist.
4. Let salmon cool slightly, remove skin and cut into 4 portions.
5. Divide lettuce, asparagus and tomatoes among 4 plates.
6. Top each salad with a salmon portion and drizzle with dressing.
7. Serve with extra dressing on the side.

Variations & Ingredients Tips:

▶ Use any fresh herb like dill, parsley or tarragon on the salmon.
▶ Substitute grilled chicken, shrimp or tofu for the salmon.
▶ Add avocado, hard boiled eggs or croutons to the salad.

Per Serving: Calories: 116; Total Fat: 3g; Saturated Fat: 0.5g; Cholesterol: 35mg; Sodium: 180mg; Total Carbs: 6g; Dietary Fiber: 3g; Total Sugars: 2g; Protein: 16g

Roasted Ratatouille Vegetables

Cooking Time: 15 Minutes | Prep Time: 10 Minutes | Servings: 2

Ingredients:

- 1 baby or Japanese eggplant, cut into 3.5cm cubes
- 1 red pepper, cut into 2.5cm chunks
- 1 yellow pepper, cut into 2.5cm chunks
- 1 zucchini, cut into 2.5cm chunks
- 1 garlic clove, minced
- 1/2 teaspoon dried basil
- 1 tablespoon olive oil
- Salt and freshly ground black pepper
- 1/4 cup sliced sun-dried tomatoes in oil
- 2 tablespoons chopped fresh basil

Directions:

1. Preheat air fryer to 200°C/400°F.
2. Toss eggplant, peppers, zucchini, garlic, dried basil, olive oil, salt and pepper in a bowl.
3. Air fry veggies at 200°C/400°F for 15 minutes, shaking basket a few times.
4. When tender, toss immediately with sun-dried tomatoes and fresh basil.
5. Serve.

Variations & Ingredients Tips:

▶ Add halved cherry tomatoes before roasting.
▶ Drizzle with balsamic glaze or lemon juice after roasting.
▶ Sprinkle with parmesan or feta cheese.

Per Serving: Calories: 156; Total Fat: 11g; Saturated Fat: 1g; Cholesterol: 0mg; Sodium: 69mg; Total Carbohydrates: 13g; Dietary Fiber: 5g; Total Sugars: 8g; Protein: 3g

Roasted Herbed Shiitake Mushrooms

Cooking Time: 5 Minutes | Prep Time: 5 Minutes | Servings: 4

Ingredients:

- 227g shiitake mushrooms, stemmed and caps chopped
- 1 tablespoon olive oil
- 1/2 teaspoon salt
- Freshly ground black pepper
- 1 teaspoon chopped fresh thyme
- 1 teaspoon chopped fresh oregano
- 1 tablespoon chopped fresh parsley

Directions:

1. Preheat air fryer to 200°C/400°F.
2. In a bowl, toss mushrooms with olive oil, salt, pepper, thyme and oregano.
3. Transfer mushrooms to air fryer basket and cook for 5 minutes, shaking basket 1-2 times.
4. For more tender mushrooms, increase cook time by 2 minutes.
5. Once cooked, toss mushrooms with chopped parsley.
6. Season again to taste and serve.

Variations & Ingredients Tips:

▶ Use a blend of wild mushroom varieties.
▶ Add minced garlic or shallots before roasting.

▶ Finish with a squeeze of lemon juice.

Per Serving: Calories: 55; Total Fat: 4g; Saturated Fat: 1g; Cholesterol: 0mg; Sodium: 234mg; Total Carbohydrates: 4g; Dietary Fiber: 1g; Total Sugars: 2g; Protein: 2g

Baked Shishito Peppers

Servings: 2 | Prep Time: 5 Minutes | Cooking Time: 15 Minutes

Ingredients:

- 170g shishito peppers
- 1 tsp olive oil
- 1 tsp salt
- ¼ cup soy sauce

Directions:

1. Preheat air fryer at 190°C/375°F.
2. Combine all ingredients in a bowl.
3. Place peppers in the frying basket and Bake for 8 minutes until the peppers are blistered, shaking once.
4. Serve with soy sauce for dipping.

Variations & Ingredients Tips:

▶ Toss with lemon juice and parmesan after baking.
▶ Sprinkle with togarashi or chili powder for extra heat.
▶ Substitute ponzu sauce for the soy sauce.

Per Serving: Calories: 52; Total Fat: 3g; Saturated Fat: 0g; Cholesterol: 0mg; Sodium: 1225mg; Total Carbs: 6g; Fiber: 2g; Sugars: 3g; Protein: 2g

Glazed Carrots

Servings: 4 | Prep Time: 5 Minutes | Cooking Time: 10 Minutes

Ingredients:

- 2 teaspoons honey
- 1 teaspoon orange juice
- 1/2 teaspoon grated orange rind
- 1/8 teaspoon ginger
- 454g baby carrots
- 2 teaspoons olive oil
- 1/4 teaspoon salt

Directions:

1. Combine honey, orange juice, grated rind, and ginger in a small bowl and set aside.
2. Toss the carrots, oil, and salt together to coat well and pour them into the air fryer basket.
3. Cook at 200°C/390°F for 5 minutes. Shake basket to stir a little and cook for 4 minutes more, until carrots are barely tender.
4. Pour carrots into air fryer baking pan.
5. Stir the honey mixture to combine well, pour glaze over carrots, and stir to coat.
6. Cook at 182°C/360°F for 1 minute or just until heated through.

Variations & Ingredients Tips:

- For extra flavor, add a pinch of cinnamon or nutmeg to the glaze.
- Swap orange juice for lemon or lime juice.
- Use maple syrup instead of honey.

Per Serving: Calories: 90; Total Fat: 2.5g; Saturated Fat: 0g; Cholesterol: 0mg; Sodium: 200mg; Total Carbohydrates: 16g; Dietary Fiber: 3g; Total Sugars: 11g; Protein: 1g

Sweet Potato Curly Fries

Servings: 4 | Prep Time: 10 Minutes | Cooking Time: 10 Minutes

Ingredients:

- 2 medium sweet potatoes, washed
- 2 tablespoons avocado oil
- ¾ teaspoon salt, divided
- 1 medium avocado
- ½ teaspoon garlic powder
- ½ teaspoon paprika
- ¼ teaspoon black pepper
- ½ juice lime
- 3 tablespoons fresh cilantro

Directions:

1. Preheat the air fryer to 200°C/400°F.
2. Using a spiralizer, create curly spirals with the sweet potatoes. Keep the pieces about 4 cm long. Continue until all the potatoes are used.
3. In a large bowl, toss the curly sweet potatoes with the avocado oil and ½ teaspoon of the salt.
4. Place the potatoes in the air fryer basket and cook for 5 minutes; shake and cook another 5 minutes.
5. While cooking, add the avocado, garlic, paprika, pepper, the remaining ¼ teaspoon of salt, lime juice, and cilantro to a blender and process until smooth. Set aside.
6. When cooking completes, remove the fries and serve warm with the lime avocado sauce.

Variations & Ingredients Tips:

- Use different types of potatoes, such as russet or Yukon Gold, for a variety of flavors and textures.
- Add some chili powder or cayenne pepper to the spice mixture for a spicy kick.
- Serve the fries with different dipping sauces, such as ranch dressing or ketchup.

Per Serving: Calories: 200; Total Fat: 12g; Saturated Fat: 2g; Cholesterol: 0mg; Sodium: 440mg; Total Carbs: 23g; Fiber: 5g; Sugars: 5g; Protein: 2g

Brown Rice And Goat Cheese Croquettes

Servings: 3 | Prep Time: 15 Minutes | Cooking Time: 8 Minutes

Ingredients:

- ¾ cup Water
- 6 tablespoons Raw medium-grain brown rice, such as brown Arborio
- ½ cup Shredded carrot
- ¼ cup Walnut pieces
- 3 tablespoons (about 43g) Soft goat cheese
- 1 tablespoon Pasteurized egg substitute, such as Egg Beaters (gluten-free, if a concern)
- ¼ teaspoon Dried thyme
- ¼ teaspoon Table salt
- ¼ teaspoon Ground black pepper
- Olive oil spray

Directions:

1. Combine the water, rice, and carrots in a small saucepan set over medium-high heat. Bring to a boil, stirring occasionally. Cover, reduce the heat to very low, and simmer very slowly for 45 minutes, or until the water has been absorbed and the rice is tender. Set aside, covered, for 10 minutes.
2. Scrape the contents of the saucepan into a food processor. Cool for 10 minutes.
3. Preheat the air fryer to 200°C/400°F.
4. Put the nuts, cheese, egg substitute, thyme, salt, and pepper into the food processor. Cover and pulse to a coarse paste, stopping the machine at least once to

scrape down the inside of the canister.

5. Uncover the food processor; scrape down and remove the blade. Using wet, clean hands, form the mixture into two 10cm-diameter patties for a small batch, three 10cm-diameter patties for a medium batch, or four 10cm-diameter patties for a large one. Generously coat both sides of the patties with olive oil spray.
6. Set the patties in the basket with as much air space between them as possible. Air-fry undisturbed for 8 minutes, or until brown and crisp.
7. Use a nonstick-safe spatula to transfer the croquettes to a wire rack. Cool for 5 minutes before serving.

Variations & Ingredients Tips:

- Substitute different grains like quinoa or farro for the brown rice.
- Add finely chopped spinach or kale to the mixture.
- Serve with a yogurt dill sauce for dipping.

Per Serving: Calories: 225; Total Fat: 10g; Saturated Fat: 3g; Cholesterol: 5mg; Sodium: 330mg; Total Carbs: 27g; Fiber: 3g; Sugars: 2g; Protein: 8g

Sandwiches And Burgers Recipes

Philly Cheesesteak Sandwiches

Servings: 3 | Prep Time: 10 Minutes | Cooking Time: 9 Minutes

Ingredients:

- 340 grams Shaved beef
- 1 tablespoon Worcestershire sauce (gluten-free, if a concern)
- ¼ teaspoon Garlic powder
- ¼ teaspoon Mild paprika
- 6 tablespoons (45 grams) Frozen bell pepper strips (do not thaw)
- 2 slices, broken into rings Very thin yellow or white medium onion slice(s)
- 170 grams (6 to 8 slices) Provolone cheese slices
- 3 Long soft rolls such as hero, hoagie, or Italian sub rolls, or hot dog buns (gluten-free, if a concern), split open lengthwise

Directions:

1. Preheat the air fryer to 200°C/400°F.
2. When the machine is at temperature, spread the shaved beef in the basket, leaving a 1.25-cm perimeter around the meat for good air flow. Sprinkle the meat with the Worcestershire sauce, paprika, and garlic powder. Spread the peppers and onions on top of the meat.
3. Air-fry undisturbed for 6 minutes, or until cooked through. Set the cheese on top of the meat. Continue air-frying undisturbed for 3 minutes, or until the cheese has melted.
4. Use kitchen tongs to divide the meat and cheese layers in the basket between the rolls or buns. Serve hot.

Variations & Ingredients Tips:

- Use thinly sliced ribeye or sirloin steak instead of shaved beef for a more traditional texture.
- Add sliced mushrooms to the pepper and onion mixture for extra flavor and nutrition.
- Substitute provolone with American cheese or Cheez Whiz for a classic Philly taste.

Per Serving: Calories: 620; Cholesterol: 135mg; Total Fat: 32g; Saturated Fat: 15g; Sodium: 1320mg; Total Carbohydrates: 38g; Dietary Fiber: 2g; Total Sugars: 5g; Protein: 48g

Inside Out Cheeseburgers

Servings: 2 | Prep Time: 15 Minutes | Cooking Time: 20 Minutes

Ingredients:

- 340 grams lean ground beef
- 3 tablespoons minced onion
- 4 teaspoons ketchup
- 2 teaspoons yellow mustard
- salt and freshly ground black pepper
- 4 slices of Cheddar cheese, broken into smaller pieces
- 8 hamburger dill pickle chips

Directions:

1. Combine the ground beef, minced onion, ketchup, mustard, salt and pepper in a large bowl. Mix well to thoroughly combine the ingredients. Divide the meat into four equal portions.
2. To make the stuffed burgers, flatten each portion of meat into a thin patty. Place 4 pickle chips and half of the cheese onto the center of two of the patties, leaving a rim around the edge of the patty exposed. Place the remaining two patties on top of the first and press the meat together firmly, sealing the edges tightly. With the burgers on a flat surface, press the sides of the burger with the palm of your hand to create a straight edge. This will help keep the stuffing inside the burger while it cooks.
3. Preheat the air fryer to 190°C/370°F.
4. Place the burgers inside the air fryer basket and air-fry for 20 minutes, flipping the burgers over halfway through the cooking time.
5. Serve the cheeseburgers on buns with lettuce and tomato.

Variations & Ingredients Tips:

- Use different types of cheese like Swiss, pepper jack, or blue cheese for a unique flavor.
- Add crispy bacon pieces or sautéed mushrooms to the stuffing for extra richness.
- Brush the burgers with a mixture of melted butter and minced garlic before cooking for added flavor.

Per Serving (1 burger): Calories: 510; Cholesterol: 145mg; Total Fat: 32g; Saturated Fat: 14g; Sodium: 780mg; Total Carbohydrates: 12g; Dietary Fiber: 1g; Total Sugars: 6g; Protein: 42g

Lamb Burgers

Servings: 3 | Prep Time: 15 Minutes | Cooking Time: 17 Minutes

Ingredients:

- 510 grams Ground lamb
- 3 tablespoons Crumbled feta
- 1 teaspoon Minced garlic
- 1 teaspoon Tomato paste
- ¾ teaspoon Ground coriander
- ¾ teaspoon Ground dried ginger
- Up to ⅛ teaspoon Cayenne
- Up to a ⅛ teaspoon Table salt (optional)
- 3 Kaiser rolls or hamburger buns (gluten-free, if a concern), split open

Directions:

1. Preheat the air fryer to 190°C/375°F.
2. Gently mix the ground lamb, feta, garlic, tomato paste, coriander, ginger, cayenne, and salt (if using) in a bowl until well combined, trying to keep the bits of cheese intact. Form this mixture into two 15-cm patties for the small batch, three 12.5-cm patties for the medium, or four 12.5-cm patties for the large.
3. Set the patties in the basket in one layer and air-fry undisturbed for 16 minutes, or until an instant-read meat thermometer inserted into one burger registers 70°C/160°F. (The cheese is not an issue with the temperature probe in this recipe as it was for the Inside-Out Cheeseburgers, because the feta is so well mixed into the ground meat.)
4. Use a nonstick-safe spatula, and perhaps a flatware fork for balance, to transfer the burgers to a cutting board. Set the buns cut side down in the basket in one layer (working in batches as necessary) and air-fry undisturbed for 1 minute, to toast a bit and warm up. Serve the burgers warm in the buns.

Variations & Ingredients Tips:

- Substitute feta with goat cheese or crumbled blue cheese for a different flavor profile.
- Add finely chopped mint or parsley to the lamb mixture for a fresh, herbal taste.
- Serve with tzatziki sauce, sliced cucumbers, and red onions for a Greek-inspired burger.

Per Serving (1 burger): Calories: 560; Cholesterol: 140mg; Total Fat: 34g; Saturated Fat: 15g; Sodium: 580mg; Total Carbohydrates: 25g; Dietary Fiber: 1g; Total Sugars: 3g; Protein: 38g

Dijon Thyme Burgers

Servings: 3 | Prep Time: 15 Minutes | Cooking Time: 18 Minutes

Ingredients:

- 450 grams lean ground beef
- ⅓ cup panko breadcrumbs
- ¼ cup finely chopped onion
- 3 tablespoons Dijon mustard
- 1 tablespoon chopped fresh thyme
- 4 teaspoons Worcestershire sauce
- 1 teaspoon salt
- freshly ground black pepper
- Topping (optional):
- 2 tablespoons Dijon mustard
- 1 tablespoon dark brown sugar
- 1 teaspoon Worcestershire sauce
- 115 grams sliced Swiss cheese, optional

Directions:

1. Combine all the burger ingredients together in a large bowl and mix well. Divide the meat into 4 equal portions and then form the burgers, being careful not to over-handle the meat. One good way to do this is to throw the meat back and forth from one hand to another, packing the meat each time you catch it. Flatten the balls into patties, making an indentation in the center of each patty with your thumb (this will help it stay flat as it cooks) and flattening the sides of the burgers so that they will fit nicely into the air fryer basket.
2. Preheat the air fryer to 190°C/370°F.
3. If you don't have room for all four burgers, air-fry two or three burgers at a time for 8 minutes. Flip the burgers over and air-fry for another 6 minutes.
4. While the burgers are cooking combine the Dijon mustard, dark brown sugar, and Worcestershire sauce in a small bowl and mix well. This optional topping to the burgers really adds a boost of flavor at the end. Spread the Dijon topping evenly on each burger. If you cooked the burgers in batches, return the first batch to the cooker at this time – it's ok to place the fourth burger on top of the others in the center of the basket. Air-fry the burgers for another 3 minutes.
5. Finally, if desired, top each burger with a slice of Swiss cheese. Lower the air fryer temperature to 165°C/330°F and air-fry for another minute to melt the cheese. Serve the burgers on toasted brioche buns, dressed the way you like them.

Variations & Ingredients Tips:

- Use ground turkey or chicken for a leaner burger option.
- Add minced garlic or finely chopped herbs like parsley or chives for extra flavor.
- Substitute panko breadcrumbs with regular breadcrumbs or oats for a different texture.

Per Serving (1 burger with cheese): Calories: 500; Cholesterol: 120mg; Total Fat: 27g; Saturated Fat: 11g; Sodium: 1180mg; Total Carbohydrates: 21g; Dietary Fiber: 1g; Total Sugars: 5g; Protein: 41g

Thanksgiving Turkey Sandwiches

Servings: 3 | Prep Time: 15 Minutes | Cooking Time: 10 Minutes

Ingredients:

- 1½ cups Herb-seasoned stuffing mix (not cornbread-style; gluten-free, if a concern)
- 1 Large egg white(s)
- 2 tablespoons Water
- 3 140- to 170-gram turkey breast cutlets
- Vegetable oil spray
- 4½ tablespoons Purchased cranberry sauce, preferably whole berry
- ⅛ teaspoon Ground cinnamon
- ⅛ teaspoon Ground dried ginger
- 4½ tablespoons Regular, low-fat, or fat-free mayonnaise (gluten-free, if a concern)
- 6 tablespoons Shredded Brussels sprouts
- 3 Kaiser rolls (gluten-free, if a concern), split open

Directions:

1. Preheat the air fryer to 190°C/375°F.
2. Put the stuffing mix in a heavy zip-closed bag, seal it, lay it flat on your counter, and roll a rolling pin over the bag to crush the stuffing mix to the consistency of rough sand. (Or you can pulse the stuffing mix to the desired consistency in a food processor.)
3. Set up and fill two shallow soup plates or small pie plates on your counter: one for the egg white(s), whisked with the water until foamy; and one for the ground stuffing mix.
4. Dip a cutlet in the egg white mixture, coating both sides and letting any excess egg white slip back into the rest. Set the cutlet in the ground stuffing mix and coat it evenly on both sides, pressing gently to coat well on both sides. Lightly coat the cutlet on both sides with vegetable oil spray, set it aside, and continue dipping and coating the remaining cutlets in the same way.
5. Set the cutlets in the basket and air-fry undisturbed for 10 minutes, or until crisp and brown. Use kitchen tongs to transfer the cutlets to a wire rack to cool for a

few minutes.

6. Meanwhile, stir the cranberry sauce with the cinnamon and ginger in a small bowl. Mix the shredded Brussels sprouts and mayonnaise in a second bowl until the vegetable is evenly coated.
7. Build the sandwiches by spreading about 1½ tablespoons of the cranberry mixture on the cut side of the bottom half of each roll. Set a cutlet on top, then spread about 3 tablespoons of the Brussels sprouts mixture evenly over the cutlet. Set the other half of the roll on top and serve warm.

Variations & Ingredients Tips:

▸ Use leftover roasted turkey instead of turkey cutlets for a post-Thanksgiving sandwich.
▸ Substitute Brussels sprouts with shredded cabbage or kale for a different texture and flavor.
▸ Add a slice of brie or provolone cheese to the sandwich for extra creaminess.

Per Serving: Calories: 530; Cholesterol: 75mg; Total Fat: 22g; Saturated Fat: 4g; Sodium: 1180mg; Total Carbohydrates: 53g; Dietary Fiber: 4g; Total Sugars: 15g; Protein: 33g

Chili Cheese Dogs

Servings: 3 | Prep Time: 10 Minutes | Cooking Time: 12 Minutes

Ingredients:

- 340 grams Lean ground beef
- 1½ tablespoons Chile powder
- 240 grams plus 2 tablespoons Jarred sofrito
- 3 Hot dogs (gluten-free, if a concern)
- 3 Hot dog buns (gluten-free, if a concern), split open lengthwise
- 3 tablespoons Finely chopped scallion
- 60 grams Shredded Cheddar cheese

Directions:

1. Crumble the ground beef into a medium or large saucepan set over medium heat. Brown well, stirring often to break up the clumps. Add the chile powder and cook for 30 seconds, stirring the whole time. Stir in the sofrito and bring to a simmer. Reduce the heat to low and simmer, stirring occasionally, for 5 minutes. Keep warm.
2. Preheat the air fryer to 200°C/400°F.
3. When the machine is at temperature, put the hot dogs in the basket and air-fry undisturbed for 10 minutes, or until the hot dogs are bubbling and blistered, even a little crisp.
4. Use kitchen tongs to put the hot dogs in the buns. Top each with about 120 grams of the ground beef mixture, 1 tablespoon of the minced scallion, and 20 grams of the cheese. (The scallion should go under the cheese so it superheats and wilts a bit.) Set the filled hot dog buns in the basket and air-fry undisturbed for 2 minutes, or until the cheese has melted.
5. Remove the basket from the machine. Cool the chili cheese dogs in the basket for 5 minutes before serving.

Variations & Ingredients Tips:

▸ Use turkey or veggie hot dogs for a healthier option.
▸ Substitute cheddar cheese with your favorite melty cheese, such as pepper jack or Swiss.
▸ Add diced onions or jalapeños to the chili for extra flavor and heat.

Per Serving: Calories: 580; Cholesterol: 110mg; Total Fat: 32g; Saturated Fat: 13g; Sodium: 1420mg; Total Carbohydrates: 36g; Dietary Fiber: 5g; Total Sugars: 6g; Protein: 38g

Black Bean Veggie Burgers

Servings: 3 | Prep Time: 15 Minutes | Cooking Time: 10 Minutes

Ingredients:

- 1 cup Drained and rinsed canned black beans
- ⅓ cup Pecan pieces
- ⅓ cup Rolled oats (not quick-cooking or steel-cut; gluten-free, if a concern)
- 2 tablespoons (or 1 small egg) Pasteurized egg substitute, such as Egg Beaters (gluten-free, if a concern)
- 2 teaspoons Red ketchup-like chili sauce, such as Heinz
- ¼ teaspoon Ground cumin
- ¼ teaspoon Dried oregano
- ¼ teaspoon Table salt
- ¼ teaspoon Ground black pepper
- Olive oil
- Olive oil spray

Directions:

1. Preheat the air fryer to 200°C/400°F.
2. Put the beans, pecans, oats, egg substitute or egg, chili

sauce, cumin, oregano, salt, and pepper in a food processor. Cover and process to a coarse paste that will hold its shape like sugar-cookie dough, adding olive oil in 1-teaspoon increments to get the mixture to blend smoothly. The amount of olive oil is actually dependent on the internal moisture content of the beans and the oats. Figure on about 1 tablespoon (three 1-teaspoon additions) for the smaller batch, with proportional increases for the other batches. A little too much olive oil can't hurt, but a dry paste will fall apart as it cooks and a far-too-wet paste will stick to the basket.
3. Scrape down and remove the blade. Using clean, wet hands, form the paste into two 10 cm patties for the small batch, three 10 cm patties for the medium, or four 10 cm patties for the large batch, setting them one by one on a cutting board. Generously coat both sides of the patties with olive oil spray.
4. Set them in the basket in one layer. Air-fry undisturbed for 10 minutes, or until lightly browned and crisp at the edges.
5. Use a nonstick-safe spatula, and perhaps a flatware fork for balance, to transfer the burgers to a wire rack. Cool for 5 minutes before serving.

Variations & Ingredients Tips:

- Add finely chopped vegetables like bell peppers, onions, or carrots for extra flavor and nutrition.
- Experiment with different spices and herbs, such as smoked paprika, garlic powder, or cilantro.
- For a gluten-free version, ensure all ingredients are certified gluten-free.

Per Serving: Calories: 280; Cholesterol: 0mg; Total Fat: 15g; Saturated Fat: 2g; Sodium: 420mg; Total Carbohydrates: 28g; Dietary Fiber: 8g; Total Sugars: 2g; Protein: 10g

Salmon Burgers

Servings: 3 | Prep Time: 15 Minutes | Cooking Time: 8 Minutes

Ingredients:

- 510 grams Skinless salmon fillet, preferably fattier Atlantic salmon
- 1½ tablespoons Minced chives or the green part of a scallion
- ½ cup Plain panko bread crumbs (gluten-free, if a concern)
- 1½ teaspoons Dijon mustard (gluten-free, if a concern)
- 1½ teaspoons Drained and rinsed capers, minced
- 1½ teaspoons Lemon juice
- ¼ teaspoon Table salt
- ¼ teaspoon Ground black pepper
- Vegetable oil spray

Directions:

1. Preheat the air fryer to 190°C/375°F.
2. Cut the salmon into pieces that will fit in a food processor. Cover and pulse until coarsely chopped. Add the chives and pulse to combine, until the fish is ground but not a paste. Scrape down and remove the blade. Scrape the salmon mixture into a bowl. Add the bread crumbs, mustard, capers, lemon juice, salt, and pepper. Stir gently until well combined.
3. Use clean and dry hands to form the mixture into two 12.5-cm patties for a small batch, three 12.5-cm patties for a medium batch, or four 12.5-cm patties for a large one.
4. Coat both sides of each patty with vegetable oil spray. Set them in the basket in one layer and air-fry undisturbed for 8 minutes, or until browned and an instant-read meat thermometer inserted into the center of a burger registers 65°C/145°F.
5. Use a nonstick-safe spatula, and perhaps a flatware fork for balance, to transfer the burgers to a wire rack. Cool for 2 or 3 minutes before serving.

Variations & Ingredients Tips:

- Substitute salmon with canned or leftover cooked salmon for convenience.
- Add finely chopped red bell pepper or celery to the burger mixture for extra crunch and flavor.
- Serve on toasted buns with lettuce, tomato, and a dollop of tartar sauce or remoulade.

Per Serving (1 burger): Calories: 320; Cholesterol: 95mg; Total Fat: 16g; Saturated Fat: 3g; Sodium: 440mg; Total Carbohydrates: 15g; Dietary Fiber: 1g; Total Sugars: 1g; Protein: 31g

Asian Glazed Meatballs

Servings: 4 | Prep Time: 15 Minutes | Cooking Time: 10 Minutes

Ingredients:

- 1 large shallot, finely chopped

- 2 cloves garlic, minced
- 1 tablespoon grated fresh ginger
- 2 teaspoons fresh thyme, finely chopped
- 1½ cups brown mushrooms, very finely chopped (a food processor works well here)
- 2 tablespoons soy sauce
- freshly ground black pepper
- ½ kg ground beef
- ¼ kg ground pork
- 3 egg yolks
- 1 cup Thai sweet chili sauce (spring roll sauce)
- ¼ cup toasted sesame seeds
- 2 scallions, sliced

Directions:

1. Combine the shallot, garlic, ginger, thyme, mushrooms, soy sauce, freshly ground black pepper, ground beef and pork, and egg yolks in a bowl and mix the ingredients together. Gently shape the mixture into 24 balls, about the size of a golf ball.
2. Preheat the air fryer to 190°C/380°F.
3. Working in batches, air-fry the meatballs for 8 minutes, turning the meatballs over halfway through the cooking time. Drizzle some of the Thai sweet chili sauce on top of each meatball and return the basket to the air fryer, air-frying for another 2 minutes. Reserve the remaining Thai sweet chili sauce for serving.
4. As soon as the meatballs are done, sprinkle with toasted sesame seeds and transfer them to a serving platter. Scatter the scallions around and serve warm.

Variations & Ingredients Tips:

- Use a food processor to finely chop the mushrooms for better texture in the meatballs.
- Work in batches when air frying the meatballs to ensure even cooking and browning.
- Drizzle the Thai sweet chili sauce over the meatballs towards the end of cooking for a nice glaze.

Per Serving: Calories: 550; Cholesterol: 205mg; Total Fat: 32g; Saturated Fat: 11g; Sodium: 1300mg; Total Carbohydrates: 36g; Dietary Fiber: 2g; Total Sugars: 23g; Protein: 29g

Mexican Cheeseburgers

Servings: 4 | Prep Time: 20 Minutes | Cooking Time: 22 Minutes

Ingredients:

- 570 grams ground beef
- ¼ cup finely chopped onion
- ½ cup crushed yellow corn tortilla chips
- 1 (35-gram) packet taco seasoning
- ¼ cup canned diced green chilies
- 1 egg, lightly beaten
- 115 grams pepper jack cheese, grated
- 4 (30-cm) flour tortillas
- shredded lettuce, sour cream, guacamole, salsa (for topping)

Directions:

1. Combine the ground beef, minced onion, crushed tortilla chips, taco seasoning, green chilies, and egg in a large bowl. Mix thoroughly until combined – your hands are good tools for this. Divide the meat into four equal portions and shape each portion into an oval-shaped burger.
2. Preheat the air fryer to 190°C/370°F.
3. Air-fry the burgers for 18 minutes, turning them over halfway through the cooking time. Divide the cheese between the burgers, lower fryer to 170°C/340°F and air-fry for an additional 4 minutes to melt the cheese. (This will give you a burger that is medium-well. If you prefer your cheeseburger medium-rare, shorten the cooking time to about 15 minutes and then add the cheese and proceed with the recipe.)
4. While the burgers are cooking, warm the tortillas wrapped in aluminum foil in a 175°C/350°F oven, or in a skillet with a little oil over medium-high heat for a couple of minutes. Keep the tortillas warm until the burgers are ready.
5. To assemble the burgers, spread sour cream over three quarters of the tortillas and top each with some shredded lettuce and salsa. Place the Mexican cheeseburgers on the lettuce and top with guacamole. Fold the tortillas around the burger, starting with the bottom and then folding the sides in over the top. (A little sour cream can help hold the seam of the tortilla together.) Serve immediately.

Variations & Ingredients Tips:

- Use ground turkey or chicken for a leaner burger option.
- Substitute pepper jack cheese with Monterey Jack or cheddar cheese if preferred.
- Add sliced jalapeños or hot sauce to the burger mixture for extra heat.

Per Serving (1 burger): Calories: 780; Cholesterol: 165mg; Total Fat: 44g; Saturated Fat: 18g; Sodium:

1480mg; Total Carbohydrates: 51g; Dietary Fiber: 4g; Total Sugars: 4g; Protein: 46g

White Bean Veggie Burgers

Servings: 3 | Prep Time: 15 Minutes | Cooking Time: 13 Minutes

Ingredients:

- 320 grams Drained and rinsed canned white beans
- 3 tablespoons Rolled oats (not quick-cooking or steel-cut; gluten-free, if a concern)
- 3 tablespoons Chopped walnuts
- 2 teaspoons Olive oil
- 2 teaspoons Lemon juice
- 1½ teaspoons Dijon mustard (gluten-free, if a concern)
- ¾ teaspoon Dried sage leaves
- ¼ teaspoon Table salt
- Olive oil spray
- 3 Whole-wheat buns or gluten-free whole-grain buns (if a concern), split open

Directions:

1. Preheat the air fryer to 200°C/400°F.
2. Place the beans, oats, walnuts, oil, lemon juice, mustard, sage, and salt in a food processor. Cover and process to make a coarse paste that will hold its shape, about like wet sugar-cookie dough, stopping the machine to scrape down the inside of the canister at least once.
3. Scrape down and remove the blade. With clean and wet hands, form the bean paste into two 10-cm patties for the small batch, three 10-cm patties for the medium, or four 10-cm patties for the large batch. Generously coat the patties on both sides with olive oil spray.
4. Set them in the basket with some space between them and air-fry undisturbed for 12 minutes, or until lightly brown and crisp at the edges. The tops of the burgers will feel firm to the touch.
5. Use a nonstick-safe spatula, and perhaps a flatware fork for balance, to transfer the burgers to a cutting board. Set the buns cut side down in the basket in one layer (working in batches as necessary) and air-fry undisturbed for 1 minute, to toast a bit and warm up. Serve the burgers warm in the buns.

Variations & Ingredients Tips:

- Use black beans, chickpeas, or lentils instead of white beans for a different flavor and color.
- Add grated carrots, zucchini, or beets to the burger mixture for extra nutrition and texture.
- Serve with your favorite burger toppings like lettuce, tomato, onion, and pickles.

Per Serving (1 burger): Calories: 350; Cholesterol: 0mg; Total Fat: 13g; Saturated Fat: 1g; Sodium: 520mg; Total Carbohydrates: 48g; Dietary Fiber: 9g; Total Sugars: 4g; Protein: 14g

Inside-out Cheeseburgers

Servings: 3 | Prep Time: 15 Minutes | Cooking Time: 9-11 Minutes

Ingredients:

- 510 grams 90% lean ground beef
- ¾ teaspoon Dried oregano
- ¾ teaspoon Table salt
- ¾ teaspoon Ground black pepper
- ¼ teaspoon Garlic powder
- 6 tablespoons (about 45 grams) Shredded Cheddar, Swiss, or other semi-firm cheese, or a purchased blend of shredded cheeses
- 3 Hamburger buns (gluten-free, if a concern), split open

Directions:

1. Preheat the air fryer to 190°C/375°F.
2. Gently mix the ground beef, oregano, salt, pepper, and garlic powder in a bowl until well combined without turning the mixture to mush. Form it into two 15-cm patties for the small batch, three for the medium, or four for the large.
3. Place 2 tablespoons of the shredded cheese in the center of each patty. With clean hands, fold the sides of the patty up to cover the cheese, then pick it up and roll it gently into a ball to seal the cheese inside. Gently press it back into a 12.5-cm burger without letting any cheese squish out. Continue filling and preparing more burgers, as needed.
4. Place the burgers in the basket in one layer and air-fry undisturbed for 8 minutes for medium or 10 minutes for well-done. (An instant-read meat thermometer won't work for these burgers because it will hit the mostly melted cheese inside and offer a hotter temperature than the surrounding meat.)
5. Use a nonstick-safe spatula, and perhaps a flatware fork for balance, to transfer the burgers to a cutting board. Set the buns cut side down in the basket in one

layer (working in batches as necessary) and air-fry undisturbed for 1 minute, to toast a bit and warm up. Cool the burgers a few minutes more, then serve them warm in the buns.

Variations & Ingredients Tips:

- Mix different types of cheese like cheddar, mozzarella, and blue cheese for a flavorful combination.
- Add finely chopped bacon or caramelized onions to the cheese stuffing for extra richness.
- Serve with your favorite burger toppings like lettuce, tomato, onion, and pickles.

Per Serving (1 burger): Calories: 480; Cholesterol: 125mg; Total Fat: 27g; Saturated Fat: 11g; Sodium: 720mg; Total Carbohydrates: 22g; Dietary Fiber: 1g; Total Sugars: 3g; Protein: 38g

Chicken Gyros

Servings: 4 | Prep Time: 10 Minutes (plus Marinating Time) | Cooking Time: 14 Minutes

Ingredients:

- 4 110to 140-gram boneless skinless chicken thighs, trimmed of any fat blobs
- 2 tablespoons Lemon juice
- 2 tablespoons Red wine vinegar
- 2 tablespoons Olive oil
- 2 teaspoons Dried oregano
- 2 teaspoons Minced garlic
- 1 teaspoon Table salt
- 1 teaspoon Ground black pepper
- 4 Pita pockets (gluten-free, if a concern)
- ½ cup Chopped tomatoes
- ½ cup Bottled regular, low-fat, or fat-free ranch dressing (gluten-free, if a concern)

Directions:

1. Mix the thighs, lemon juice, vinegar, oil, oregano, garlic, salt, and pepper in a zip-closed bag. Seal, gently massage the marinade into the meat through the plastic, and refrigerate for at least 2 hours or up to 6 hours. (Longer than that and the meat can turn rubbery.)
2. Set the plastic bag out on the counter (to make the contents a little less frigid). Preheat the air fryer to 190°C/375°F.
3. When the machine is at temperature, use kitchen tongs to place the thighs in the basket in one layer. Discard the marinade. Air-fry the chicken thighs undisturbed for 12 minutes, or until browned and an instant-read meat thermometer inserted into the thickest part of one thigh registers 75°C/165°F. You may need to air-fry the chicken 2 minutes longer if the machine's temperature is 70°C/360°F.
4. Use kitchen tongs to transfer the thighs to a cutting board. Cool for 5 minutes, then set one thigh in each of the pita pockets. Top each with 2 tablespoons chopped tomatoes and 2 tablespoons dressing. Serve warm.

Variations & Ingredients Tips:

- Substitute chicken thighs with chicken breast for a leaner option.
- Add shredded lettuce, sliced onions, or cucumbers for extra crunch and flavor.
- Use homemade tzatziki sauce instead of ranch dressing for a more authentic taste.

Per Serving: Calories: 460; Cholesterol: 95mg; Total Fat: 28g; Saturated Fat: 5g; Sodium: 1070mg; Total Carbohydrates: 29g; Dietary Fiber: 2g; Total Sugars: 4g; Protein: 25g

Chicken Spiedies

Servings: 3 | Prep Time: 15 Minutes (plus Marinating Time) | Cooking Time: 12 Minutes

Ingredients:

- 570 grams Boneless skinless chicken thighs, trimmed of any fat blobs and cut into 5-cm pieces
- 3 tablespoons Red wine vinegar
- 2 tablespoons Olive oil
- 2 tablespoons Minced fresh mint leaves
- 2 tablespoons Minced fresh parsley leaves
- 2 teaspoons Minced fresh dill fronds
- ¾ teaspoon Fennel seeds
- ¾ teaspoon Table salt
- Up to a ¼ teaspoon Red pepper flakes
- 3 Long soft rolls, such as hero, hoagie, or Italian sub rolls (gluten-free, if a concern), split open lengthwise
- 4½ tablespoons Regular or low-fat mayonnaise (not fat-free; gluten-free, if a concern)
- 1½ tablespoons Distilled white vinegar
- 1½ teaspoons Ground black pepper

Directions:

1. Mix the chicken, vinegar, oil, mint, parsley, dill, fennel

seeds, salt, and red pepper flakes in a zip-closed plastic bag. Seal, gently massage the marinade ingredients into the meat, and refrigerate for at least 2 hours or up to 6 hours. (Longer than that and the meat can turn rubbery.)
2. Set the plastic bag out on the counter (to make the contents a little less frigid). Preheat the air fryer to 200°C/400°F.
3. When the machine is at temperature, use kitchen tongs to set the chicken thighs in the basket (discard any remaining marinade) and air-fry undisturbed for 6 minutes. Turn the thighs over and continue air-frying undisturbed for 6 minutes more, until well browned, cooked through, and even a little crunchy.
4. Dump the contents of the basket onto a wire rack and cool for 2 or 3 minutes. Divide the chicken evenly between the rolls. Whisk the mayonnaise, vinegar, and black pepper in a small bowl until smooth. Drizzle this sauce over the chicken pieces in the rolls.

Variations & Ingredients Tips:

- Use chicken breast instead of thighs for a leaner option.
- Substitute the herbs with your favorite combination, such as basil, oregano, or thyme.
- Add sliced onions or pickled vegetables for extra crunch and tanginess.

Per Serving: Calories: 710; Cholesterol: 200mg; Total Fat: 44g; Saturated Fat: 8g; Sodium: 1240mg; Total Carbohydrates: 37g; Dietary Fiber: 2g; Total Sugars: 4g; Protein: 45g

Perfect Burgers

Servings: 3 | Prep Time: 10 Minutes | Cooking Time: 13 Minutes

Ingredients:

- 510 grams 90% lean ground beef
- 1½ tablespoons Worcestershire sauce (gluten-free, if a concern)
- ½ teaspoon Ground black pepper
- 3 Hamburger buns (gluten-free if a concern), split open

Directions:

1. Preheat the air fryer to 190°C/375°F.
2. Gently mix the ground beef, Worcestershire sauce, and pepper in a bowl until well combined but preserving as much of the meat's fibers as possible. Divide this mixture into two 15-cm patties for the small batch, three 12.5-cm patties for the medium, or four 12.5-cm patties for the large. Make a thumbprint indentation in the center of each patty, about halfway through the meat.
3. Set the patties in the basket in one layer with some space between them. Air-fry undisturbed for 10 minutes, or until an instant-read meat thermometer inserted into the center of a burger registers 70°C/160°F (a medium-well burger). You may need to add 2 minutes cooking time if the air fryer is at 180°C/360°F.
4. Use a nonstick-safe spatula, and perhaps a flatware fork for balance, to transfer the burgers to a cutting board. Set the buns cut side down in the basket in one layer (working in batches as necessary) and air-fry undisturbed for 1 minute, to toast a bit and warm up. Serve the burgers in the warm buns.

Variations & Ingredients Tips:

- Mix in finely chopped onions, garlic, or herbs to the burger mixture for extra flavor.
- Use a mixture of ground beef and ground pork or lamb for a juicier, more flavorful burger.
- Top burgers with your favorite cheese, bacon, avocado, or sautéed mushrooms.

Per Serving (1 burger): Calories: 420; Cholesterol: 105mg; Total Fat: 22g; Saturated Fat: 8g; Sodium: 460mg; Total Carbohydrates: 23g; Dietary Fiber: 1g; Total Sugars: 3g; Protein: 34g

Thai-style Pork Sliders

Servings: 4 | Prep Time: 15 Minutes | Cooking Time: 15 Minutes

Ingredients:

- 310 grams Ground pork
- 2½ tablespoons Very thinly sliced scallions, white and green parts
- 4 teaspoons Minced peeled fresh ginger
- 2½ teaspoons Fish sauce (gluten-free, if a concern)
- 2 teaspoons Thai curry paste (see the headnote; gluten-free, if a concern)
- 2 teaspoons Light brown sugar
- ¾ teaspoon Ground black pepper
- 4 Slider buns (gluten-free, if a concern)

Directions:

1. Preheat the air fryer to 190°C/375°F.
2. Gently mix the pork, scallions, ginger, fish sauce, curry paste, brown sugar, and black pepper in a bowl until well combined. With clean, wet hands, form about 80 grams of the pork mixture into a slider about 6.5-cm in diameter. Repeat until you use up all the meat—3 sliders for the small batch, 4 for the medium, and 6 for the large. (Keep wetting your hands to help the patties adhere.)
3. When the machine is at temperature, set the sliders in the basket in one layer. Air-fry undisturbed for 14 minutes, or until the sliders are golden brown and caramelized at their edges and an instant-read meat thermometer inserted into the center of a slider registers 70°C/160°F.
4. Use a nonstick-safe spatula, and perhaps a flatware fork for balance, to transfer the sliders to a cutting board. Set the buns cut side down in the basket in one layer (working in batches as necessary) and air-fry undisturbed for 1 minute, to toast a bit and warm up. Serve the sliders warm in the buns.

Variations & Ingredients Tips:

- Use ground chicken or turkey for a leaner slider option.
- Substitute Thai curry paste with red curry paste or green curry paste for a different flavor profile.
- Serve with pickled vegetables, cilantro, and sriracha mayonnaise for extra Thai-inspired toppings.

Per Serving (1 slider): Calories: 240; Cholesterol: 65mg; Total Fat: 13g; Saturated Fat: 4g; Sodium: 490mg; Total Carbohydrates: 18g; Dietary Fiber: 1g; Total Sugars: 4g; Protein: 15g

Chicken Apple Brie Melt

Servings: 3 | Prep Time: 10 Minutes | Cooking Time: 13 Minutes

Ingredients:

- 3 140 to 170-gram boneless skinless chicken breasts
- Vegetable oil spray
- 1½ teaspoons Dried herbes de Provence
- 85 grams Brie, rind removed, thinly sliced
- 6 Thin cored apple slices
- 3 French rolls (gluten-free, if a concern)
- 2 tablespoons Dijon mustard (gluten-free, if a concern)

Directions:

1. Preheat the air fryer to 190°C/375°F.
2. Lightly coat all sides of the chicken breasts with vegetable oil spray. Sprinkle the breasts evenly with the herbes de Provence.
3. When the machine is at temperature, set the breasts in the basket and air-fry undisturbed for 10 minutes.
4. Top the chicken breasts with the apple slices, then the cheese. Air-fry undisturbed for 2 minutes, or until the cheese is melty and bubbling.
5. Use a nonstick-safe spatula and kitchen tongs, for balance, to transfer the breasts to a cutting board. Set the rolls in the basket and air-fry for 1 minute to warm through. (Putting them in the machine without splitting them keeps the insides very soft while the outside gets a little crunchy.)
6. Transfer the rolls to the cutting board. Split them open lengthwise, then spread 1 teaspoon mustard on each cut side. Set a prepared chicken breast on the bottom of a roll and close with its top, repeating as necessary to make additional sandwiches. Serve warm.

Variations & Ingredients Tips:

- Substitute the Brie with Camembert or another soft cheese of your choice.
- Use pears instead of apples for a different flavor profile.
- Add baby spinach or arugula for extra greens and nutrition.

Per Serving: Calories: 510; Cholesterol: 135mg; Total Fat: 19g; Saturated Fat: 8g; Sodium: 670mg; Total Carbohydrates: 41g; Dietary Fiber: 2g; Total Sugars: 6g; Protein: 45g

Provolone Stuffed Meatballs

Servings: 4 | Prep Time: 20 Minutes | Cooking Time: 12 Minutes

Ingredients:

- 1 tablespoon olive oil
- 1 small onion, very finely chopped
- 1 to 2 cloves garlic, minced
- 340 grams ground beef
- 340 grams ground pork
- ¾ cup breadcrumbs
- ¼ cup grated Parmesan cheese
- ¼ cup finely chopped fresh parsley (or 1 tablespoon dried parsley)

- ½ teaspoon dried oregano
- 1½ teaspoons salt
- freshly ground black pepper
- 2 eggs, lightly beaten
- 140 grams sharp or aged provolone cheese, cut into 2.5-cm cubes

Directions:

1. Preheat a skillet over medium-high heat. Add the oil and cook the onion and garlic until tender, but not browned.
2. Transfer the onion and garlic to a large bowl and add the beef, pork, breadcrumbs, Parmesan cheese, parsley, oregano, salt, pepper and eggs. Mix well until all the ingredients are combined. Divide the mixture into 12 evenly sized balls. Make one meatball at a time, by pressing a hole in the meatball mixture with your finger and pushing a piece of provolone cheese into the hole. Mold the meat back into a ball, enclosing the cheese.
3. Preheat the air fryer to 190°C/380°F.
4. Working in two batches, transfer six of the meatballs to the air fryer basket and air-fry for 12 minutes, shaking the basket and turning the meatballs a couple of times during the cooking process. Repeat with the remaining six meatballs. You can pop the first batch of meatballs into the air fryer for the last two minutes of cooking to re-heat them. Serve warm.

Variations & Ingredients Tips:

▶ Substitute beef and pork with ground turkey or chicken for a leaner meatball option.
▶ Use mozzarella or fontina cheese instead of provolone for a milder flavor.
▶ Serve meatballs with marinara sauce, in sub rolls, or over pasta for a complete meal.

Per Serving (3 meatballs): Calories: 520; Cholesterol: 180mg; Total Fat: 36g; Saturated Fat: 15g; Sodium: 1160mg; Total Carbohydrates: 18g; Dietary Fiber: 1g; Total Sugars: 2g; Protein: 35g

Sausage And Pepper Heros

Servings: 3 | Prep Time: 10 Minutes | Cooking Time: 11 Minutes

Ingredients:

- 3 links (about 255 grams total) Sweet Italian sausages (gluten-free, if a concern)
- 1½ Medium red or green bell pepper(s), stemmed, cored, and cut into 1.25-cm-wide strips
- 1 medium Yellow or white onion(s), peeled, halved, and sliced into thin half-moons
- 3 Long soft rolls, such as hero, hoagie, or Italian sub rolls (gluten-free, if a concern), split open lengthwise
- For garnishing Balsamic vinegar
- For garnishing Fresh basil leaves

Directions:

1. Preheat the air fryer to 200°C/400°F.
2. When the machine is at temperature, set the sausage links in the basket in one layer and air-fry undisturbed for 5 minutes.
3. Add the pepper strips and onions. Continue air-frying, tossing and rearranging everything about once every minute, for 5 minutes, or until the sausages are browned and an instant-read meat thermometer inserted into one of the links registers 70°C/160°F.
4. Use a nonstick-safe spatula and kitchen tongs to transfer the sausages and vegetables to a cutting board. Set the rolls cut side down in the basket in one layer (working in batches as necessary) and air-fry undisturbed for 1 minute, to toast the rolls a bit and warm them up. Set 1 sausage with some pepper strips and onions in each warm roll, sprinkle balsamic vinegar over the sandwich fillings, and garnish with basil leaves.

Variations & Ingredients Tips:

▶ Use hot Italian sausage or chorizo for a spicier sandwich.
▶ Add sliced mushrooms or zucchini to the pepper and onion mixture for extra veggies.
▶ Top with shredded mozzarella or provolone cheese for a cheesy twist.

Per Serving (1 sandwich): Calories: 560; Cholesterol: 60mg; Total Fat: 36g; Saturated Fat: 12g; Sodium: 1420mg; Total Carbohydrates: 39g; Dietary Fiber: 3g; Total Sugars: 7g; Protein: 24g

Crunchy Falafel Balls

Servings: 8 | Prep Time: 15 Minutes | Cooking Time: 16 Minutes

Ingredients:

- 600 grams Drained and rinsed canned chickpeas
- 60 grams Olive oil
- 3 tablespoons All-purpose flour
- 1½ teaspoons Dried oregano
- 1½ teaspoons Dried sage leaves
- 1½ teaspoons Dried thyme
- ¾ teaspoon Table salt
- Olive oil spray

Directions:

1. Preheat the air fryer to 200°C/400°F.
2. Place the chickpeas, olive oil, flour, oregano, sage, thyme, and salt in a food processor. Cover and process into a paste, stopping the machine at least once to scrape down the inside of the canister.
3. Scrape down and remove the blade. Using clean, wet hands, form 2 tablespoons of the paste into a ball, then continue making 9 more balls for a small batch, 15 more for a medium one, and 19 more for a large batch. Generously coat the balls in olive oil spray.
4. Set the balls in the basket in one layer with a little space between them and air-fry undisturbed for 16 minutes, or until well browned and crisp.
5. Dump the contents of the basket onto a wire rack. Cool for 5 minutes before serving.

Variations & Ingredients Tips:

- Add minced garlic, onion, or herbs like parsley or cilantro for extra flavor.
- Serve with tahini sauce, hummus, or tzatziki for dipping.
- Make a falafel sandwich by stuffing pita bread with falafel balls, lettuce, tomato, and sauce.

Per Serving (2 falafel balls): Calories: 170; Cholesterol: 0mg; Total Fat: 9g; Saturated Fat: 1g; Sodium: 230mg; Total Carbohydrates: 18g; Dietary Fiber: 4g; Total Sugars: 2g; Protein: 5g

Eggplant Parmesan Subs

Servings: 2 | Prep Time: 10 Minutes | Cooking Time: 13 Minutes

Ingredients:

- 4 Peeled eggplant slices (about 1.25 cm thick and 7.5 cm in diameter)
- Olive oil spray
- 2 tablespoons plus 2 teaspoons Jarred pizza sauce, any variety except creamy
- ¼ cup (about 20 grams) Finely grated Parmesan cheese
- 2 Small, long soft rolls, such as hero, hoagie, or Italian sub rolls (gluten-free, if a concern), split open lengthwise

Directions:

1. Preheat the air fryer to 175°C/350°F.
2. When the machine is at temperature, coat both sides of the eggplant slices with olive oil spray. Set them in the basket in one layer and air-fry undisturbed for 10 minutes, until lightly browned and softened.
3. Increase the machine's temperature to 190°C/375°F (or 185°C/370°F, if that's the closest setting—unless the machine is already at 180°C/360°F, in which case leave it alone). Top each eggplant slice with 2 teaspoons pizza sauce, then 1 tablespoon of cheese. Air-fry undisturbed for 2 minutes, or until the cheese has melted.
4. Use a nonstick-safe spatula, and perhaps a flatware fork for balance, to transfer the eggplant slices cheese side up to a cutting board. Set the roll(s) cut side down in the basket in one layer (working in batches as necessary) and air-fry undisturbed for 1 minute, to toast the rolls a bit and warm them up. Set 2 eggplant slices in each warm roll.

Variations & Ingredients Tips:

- Use zucchini slices instead of eggplant for a different vegetable option.
- Add a slice of fresh mozzarella on top of the Parmesan for extra cheesiness.
- Sprinkle some dried herbs like oregano or basil on the eggplant before cooking for extra flavor.

Per Serving (1 sandwich): Calories: 280; Cholesterol: 10mg; Total Fat: 9g; Saturated Fat: 3g; Sodium: 840mg; Total Carbohydrates: 40g; Dietary Fiber: 5g; Total Sugars: 8g; Protein: 11g

Desserts And Sweets

Sultana & Walnut Stuffed Apples

Servings: 4 | Prep Time: 10 Minutes | Cooking Time: 30 Minutes

Ingredients:

- 4 apples, cored and halved
- 2 tablespoons lemon juice
- 1/4 cup sultana raisins
- 3 tablespoons chopped walnuts
- 3 tablespoons dried cranberries
- 2 tablespoons packed brown sugar
- 1/3 cup apple cider
- 1 tablespoon cinnamon

Directions:

1. Preheat air fryer to 175°C/350°F.
2. Spritz the apples with lemon juice and put them in a baking pan.
3. Combine the raisins, cinnamon, walnuts, cranberries, and brown sugar, then spoon 1/4 of the mix into the apples.
4. Drizzle the apple cider around the apples, Bake for 13-18 minutes until softened.
5. Serve warm.

Variations & Ingredients Tips:

- Use other dried fruits like apricots, dates or prunes.
- Add a pinch of nutmeg or allspice to the spice mix.
- Drizzle with honey or maple syrup before serving.

Per Serving: Calories: 230; Total Fat: 6g; Saturated Fat: 1g; Cholesterol: 0mg; Sodium: 15mg; Total Carbs: 45g; Dietary Fiber: 5g; Total Sugars: 35g; Protein: 3g

Banana-lemon Bars

Servings: 6 | Prep Time: 15 Minutes | Cooking Time: 40 Minutes

Ingredients:

- 3/4 cup flour
- 2 tbsp powdered sugar
- 1/4 cup coconut oil, melted
- 1/2 cup brown sugar
- 1 tbsp lemon zest
- 1/4 cup lemon juice
- 1/8 tsp salt
- 1/4 cup mashed bananas
- 1 3/4 tsp cornstarch
- 3/4 tsp baking powder

Directions:

1. Mix flour, powdered sugar and melted coconut oil. Refrigerate.
2. Combine brown sugar, zest, juice, salt, bananas, cornstarch and baking powder.
3. Preheat air fryer to 175°C/350°F. Oil a baking pan.
4. Remove crust from fridge and press into bottom of pan. Air fry 5 mins until firm.
5. Spread lemon-banana filling over crust.
6. Bake for 18-20 mins until top is golden.
7. Cool completely before cutting into bars.

Variations & Ingredients Tips:

- Use gingersnap crumbs in the crust.
- Substitute lime juice and zest for lemon.
- Top with toasted coconut before baking.

Per Serving: Calories: 252; Total Fat: 10g; Saturated Fat: 7g; Sodium: 165mg; Total Carbohydrates: 39g; Dietary Fiber: 2g; Total Sugars: 20g; Protein: 2g

Air-fried Strawberry Hand Tarts

Servings: 9 | Prep Time: 45 Minutes | Cooking Time: 9 Minutes

Ingredients:

- ½ cup butter, softened
- ½ cup sugar
- 2 eggs
- 1 teaspoon vanilla extract
- 2 tablespoons lemon zest
- 2½ cups all-purpose flour

- 1 teaspoon baking powder
- ¼ teaspoon salt
- 1¼ cups strawberry jam, divided
- 1 egg white, beaten
- 1 cup powdered sugar
- 2 teaspoons milk

Directions:

1. Combine the butter and sugar in a bowl and beat with an electric mixer until the mixture is light and fluffy. Add the eggs one at a time. Add the vanilla extract and lemon zest and mix well.
2. In a separate bowl, combine the flour, baking powder and salt. Add the dry ingredients to the wet ingredients, mixing just until the dough comes together.
3. Transfer the dough to a floured surface and knead by hand for 10 minutes. Cover with a clean kitchen towel and let the dough rest for 30 minutes. (Alternatively, dough can be mixed and kneaded in a stand mixer.)
4. Divide the dough in half and roll each half out into a 0.6-cm thick rectangle that measures 30-cm x 23-cm. Cut each rectangle of dough into nine 10-cm x 7.5-cm rectangles (a pizza cutter is very helpful for this task). You should have 18 rectangles.
5. Spread two teaspoons of strawberry jam in the center of nine of the rectangles leaving a 0.6-cm border around the edges. Brush the egg white around the edges of each rectangle and top with the remaining nine rectangles of dough. Press the back of a fork around the edges to seal the tarts shut. Brush the top of the tarts with the beaten egg white and pierce the dough three or four times down the center of the tart with a fork.
6. Preheat the air fryer to 180°C/350°F.
7. Air-fry the tarts in batches at 180°C/350°F for 6 minutes. Flip the tarts over and air-fry for an additional 3 minutes.
8. While the tarts are air-frying, make the icing. Combine the powdered sugar, ¼ cup strawberry preserves and milk in a bowl, whisking until the icing is smooth.
9. Spread the icing over the top of each tart, leaving an empty border around the edges. Decorate with sprinkles if desired.

Variations & Ingredients Tips:

▶ Substitute strawberry jam with raspberry, blueberry, or apricot preserves.
▶ Add a pinch of ground cinnamon or nutmeg to the dough for extra flavor.
▶ Drizzle with melted white or dark chocolate instead of icing.

Per Serving: Calories: 410; Total Fat: 14g; Saturated Fat: 8g; Sodium: 200mg; Total Carbohydrates: 68g; Dietary Fiber: 1g; Total Sugars: 40g; Protein: 5g

Dark Chocolate Cream Galette

Servings: 4 | Prep Time: 15 Minutes | Cooking Time: 55 Minutes + Cooling Time

Ingredients:

- 454 grams cream cheese, softened
- 1 cup crumbled graham crackers
- 1 cup dark cocoa powder
- ½ cup white sugar
- 1 tsp peppermint extract
- 1 tsp ground cinnamon
- 1 egg
- 1 cup condensed milk
- 2 tbsp muscovado sugar
- 1 ½ tsp butter, melted

Directions:

1. Preheat air fryer to 180°C/350°F.
2. Place the crumbled graham crackers in a large bowl and stir in the muscovado sugar and melted butter. Spread the mixture into a greased pie pan, pressing down to form the galette base.
3. Place the pan into the air fryer and Bake for 5 minutes. Remove the pan and set aside.
4. Place the cocoa powder, cream cheese, peppermint extract, white sugar, cinnamon, condensed milk, and egg in a large bowl and whip thoroughly to combine.
5. Spoon the chocolate mixture over the graham cracker crust and level the top with a spatula. Put in the air fryer and Bake for 40 minutes until firm.
6. Transfer the galette to a wire rack to cool. Serve and enjoy!

Variations & Ingredients Tips:

▶ Use milk chocolate or white chocolate instead of dark for a sweeter flavor.
▶ Add espresso powder or instant coffee to the filling for a mocha twist.
▶ Top with fresh berries, whipped cream, or a dusting of powdered sugar.

Per Serving: Calories: 780; Total Fat: 50g; Saturated Fat: 29g; Sodium: 510mg; Total Carbohydrates: 77g; Dietary Fiber: 5g; Total Sugars: 61g; Protein: 15g

Brown Sugar Baked Apples

Servings: 4 | Prep Time: 10 Minutes | Cooking Time: 15 Minutes

Ingredients:

- 3 Small tart apples, preferably McIntosh
- 4 tablespoons (1/4 cup/1/2 stick) Butter
- 6 tablespoons Light brown sugar
- Ground cinnamon
- Table salt

Directions:

1. Preheat the air fryer to 200°C/400°F.
2. Stem the apples, then cut them in half through their "equators". Use a melon baller to core the apples, creating a cavity in the center of each half.
3. Set the apple halves cut side up in the air fryer basket with space between them.
4. Drop 2 teaspoons of butter into the cavity of each apple half.
5. Sprinkle each half with 1 tablespoon brown sugar and a pinch each of ground cinnamon and table salt.
6. Return the basket to the air fryer. Air fry for 15 minutes undisturbed, until apples are softened and brown sugar is caramelized.
7. Use a nonstick spatula to transfer apple halves cut side up to a wire rack.
8. Cool for at least 10 minutes before serving, or serve at room temperature.

Variations & Ingredients Tips:

- Use a mix of different baking apples like Honeycrisp or Gala.
- Add chopped nuts like pecans or walnuts to the cavity.
- Drizzle with caramel sauce before serving.

Per Serving: Calories: 210; Total Fat: 9g; Saturated Fat: 5g; Sodium: 92mg; Total Carbohydrates: 33g; Dietary Fiber: 3g; Total Sugars: 27g; Protein: 1g

Air-fried Beignets

Servings: 24 | Prep Time: 20 Minutes | Cooking Time: 5 Minutes

Ingredients:

- 3/4 cup lukewarm water (about 32°C)
- 1/4 cup sugar
- 1 generous teaspoon active dry yeast (1/2 envelope)
- 3 1/2 to 4 cups all-purpose flour
- 1/2 teaspoon salt
- 2 tablespoons unsalted butter, room temperature and cut into small pieces
- 1 egg, lightly beaten
- 1/2 cup evaporated milk
- 1/4 cup melted butter
- 1 cup confectioners' sugar
- Chocolate sauce or raspberry sauce, to dip

Directions:

1. Combine lukewarm water, a pinch of sugar and yeast in a bowl and let proof for 5 minutes until frothy.
2. Mix 3 1/2 cups flour, salt, 2 tbsp butter and remaining sugar in a large bowl.
3. Add egg, evaporated milk and yeast mixture and mix into a sticky dough, adding more flour if needed.
4. Let dough rise for 2 hours or overnight in the fridge.
5. Roll dough to 1.3 cm thickness and cut into rectangular or diamond shapes.
6. Preheat air fryer to 175°C/350°F.
7. Brush beignets with melted butter and air fry in batches at 175°C/350°F for 5 minutes, flipping halfway if desired.
8. Dust warm beignets with confectioners' sugar and serve with chocolate or raspberry sauce.

Variations & Ingredients Tips:

- Use bread flour for a chewier texture.
- Add ground cinnamon or nutmeg to the dough.
- Stuff with fruit preserves or cream cheese filling.

Per Serving: Calories: 132; Total Fat: 4g; Saturated Fat: 2g; Sodium: 74mg; Total Carbohydrates: 21g; Dietary Fiber: 1g; Total Sugars: 6g; Protein: 2g

Carrot-oat Cake Muffins

Servings: 4 | Prep Time: 10 Minutes | Cooking Time: 20 Minutes

Ingredients:

- 3 tbsp butter, softened
- ¼ cup brown sugar
- 1 tbsp maple syrup
- 1 egg white
- ½ tsp vanilla extract

- 1/3 cup finely grated carrots
- ½ cup oatmeal
- 1/3 cup flour
- ½ tsp baking soda
- ¼ cup raisins

Directions:

1. Preheat air fryer to 180°C/350°F.
2. Mix the butter, brown sugar, and maple syrup until smooth, then toss in the egg white, vanilla, and carrots. Whisk well and add the oatmeal, flour, baking soda, and raisins.
3. Divide the mixture between muffin cups.
4. Bake in the air fryer for 8-10 minutes.

Variations & Ingredients Tips:

- Use grated zucchini or apple instead of carrots.
- Substitute raisins with dried cranberries, chopped dates, or chocolate chips.
- Top with cream cheese frosting or a sprinkle of powdered sugar.

Per Serving: Calories: 250; Total Fat: 11g; Saturated Fat: 6g; Sodium: 230mg; Total Carbohydrates: 36g; Dietary Fiber: 2g; Total Sugars: 20g; Protein: 4g

Fried Oreos

Servings:12 | Prep Time: 15 Minutes | Cooking Time: 7 Minutes

Ingredients:

- 1 Large egg white(s)
- 2 tablespoons Water
- 1 cup Graham cracker crumbs
- 12 Original-size Oreos (not minis or king-size)
- Vegetable oil spray

Directions:

1. Preheat the air fryer to 190°C/375°F.
2. Set up and fill two shallow soup plates or small pie plates on your counter: one for the egg white(s), whisked with the water until foamy; and one for the graham cracker crumbs.
3. Dip a cookie in the egg white mixture, turning several times to coat well. Let any excess egg white mixture slip back into the rest, then set the cookie in the crumbs. Turn several times to coat evenly, pressing gently. You want an even but not thick crust. However, make sure that the cookie is fully coated and that the filling is sealed inside. Lightly coat the cookie on all sides with vegetable oil spray. Set aside and continue dipping and coating the remaining cookies.
4. Set the coated cookies in the basket with as much air space between them as possible. Air-fry undisturbed for 6 minutes, or until the coating is golden brown and set. If the machine is at 180°C/360°F, the cookies may need 1 minute more to cook and set.
5. Use a nonstick-safe spatula to transfer the cookies to a wire rack. Cool for at least 5 minutes before serving.

Variations & Ingredients Tips:

- Use different flavors of Oreos like mint, peanut butter, or birthday cake.
- Roll the cookies in cinnamon sugar instead of graham cracker crumbs.
- Serve with a scoop of vanilla ice cream or a drizzle of chocolate sauce.

Per Serving: Calories: 140; Total Fat: 7g; Saturated Fat: 2g; Sodium: 105mg; Total Carbohydrates: 19g; Dietary Fiber: 1g; Total Sugars: 11g; Protein: 1g

Banana Bread Cake

Servings: 6 | Prep Time: 15 Minutes | Cooking Time: 18-22 Minutes

Ingredients:

- 3/4 cup plus 2 tablespoons All-purpose flour
- 1/2 teaspoon Baking powder
- 1/4 teaspoon Baking soda
- 1/4 teaspoon Table salt
- 4 tablespoons (1/4 cup/1/2 stick) Butter, at room temperature
- 1/2 cup Granulated white sugar
- 2 Small ripe bananas, peeled
- 5 tablespoons Pasteurized egg substitute, such as Egg Beaters
- 1/4 cup Buttermilk
- 3/4 teaspoon Vanilla extract
- Baking spray

Directions:

1. Preheat the air fryer to 165°C/325°F (or 170°C/330°F, if that's the closest setting).
2. Mix the flour, baking powder, baking soda, and salt in a small bowl until well combined.
3. Using an electric hand mixer at medium speed, beat

the butter and sugar in a medium bowl until creamy and smooth, about 3 minutes.
4. Beat in the bananas until smooth. Then beat in egg substitute, buttermilk, and vanilla until uniform.
5. Add the flour mixture and beat at low speed until smooth and creamy.
6. Use baking spray to coat the inside of a 15cm, 18cm or 20cm round cake pan. Spread batter into the pan.
7. Set the pan in the basket and air-fry for 18 mins for 15cm, 20 mins for 18cm, or 22 mins for 20cm pan.
8. Check at 16 mins, cake is done when browned and set in center.
9. Let cool 10 mins before unmolding. Cool completely before slicing into wedges.

Variations & Ingredients Tips:

- Add chopped nuts or chocolate chips to the batter.
- Use mashed sweet potatoes or pumpkin instead of bananas.
- Top with cream cheese frosting.

Per Serving: Calories: 256; Total Fat: 10g; Saturated Fat: 6g; Sodium: 290mg; Total Carbohydrates: 37g; Dietary Fiber: 1g; Total Sugars: 18g; Protein: 4g

Vanilla Cupcakes With Chocolate Chips

Servings: 2 | Prep Time: 10 Minutes | Cooking Time: 25 Minutes + Cooling Time

Ingredients:

- 1/2 cup white sugar
- 1 1/2 cups flour
- 2 tsp baking powder
- 1/2 tsp salt
- 2/3 cup sunflower oil
- 1 egg
- 2 tsp maple extract
- 1/4 cup vanilla yogurt
- 1 cup chocolate chips

Directions:

1. Preheat air fryer to 175°C/350°F.
2. Combine the sugar, flour, baking powder, and salt in a bowl and stir to combine.
3. Whisk the egg in a separate bowl. Pour in the sunflower oil, yogurt, and maple extract, and continue whisking until light and fluffy.
4. Spoon the wet mixture into the dry ingredients and stir to combine. Gently fold in the chocolate chips with a spatula.
5. Divide the batter between cupcake cups and Bake in the air fryer for 12-15 minutes or until a toothpick comes out dry.
6. Remove the cupcakes let them cool. Serve.

Variations & Ingredients Tips:

- Use other mix-ins like nuts, dried fruit or sprinkles instead of chocolate chips.
- Top with buttercream, cream cheese or glaze frosting.
- Make into a sheet cake instead of cupcakes.

Per Serving (1 cupcake): Calories: 680; Total Fat: 40g; Saturated Fat: 6g; Cholesterol: 35mg; Sodium: 440mg; Total Carbs: 76g; Dietary Fiber: 3g; Total Sugars: 34g; Protein: 7g

Homemade Chips Ahoy

Servings: 4 | Prep Time: 10 Minutes | Cooking Time: 20 Minutes

Ingredients:

- 1 tbsp coconut oil, melted
- 1 tbsp honey
- 1 tbsp milk
- 1/2 tsp vanilla extract
- 1/4 cup oat flour
- 2 tbsp coconut sugar
- 1/4 tsp salt
- 1/4 tsp baking powder
- 2 tbsp chocolate chips

Directions:

1. Combine coconut oil, honey, milk and vanilla in a bowl.
2. Add oat flour, coconut sugar, salt and baking powder. Stir until combined.
3. Fold in chocolate chips.
4. Preheat air fryer to 175°C/350°F.
5. Pour batter into a greased baking pan, leaving some space between portions.
6. Bake for 7 minutes until golden brown. Do not overbake.
7. Transfer to a cooling rack and serve chilled.

Variations & Ingredients Tips:

- Use dairy-free milk and vegan chocolate chips for a vegan version.

- Add chopped nuts or dried fruit to the batter.
- Replace coconut sugar with brown sugar or maple syrup.

Per Serving (3 cookies): Calories: 148; Total Fat: 6g; Saturated Fat: 4g; Sodium: 116mg; Total Carbohydrates: 21g; Dietary Fiber: 2g; Total Sugars: 9g; Protein: 2g

Orange Gooey Butter Cake

Servings: 6 | Prep Time: 30 Minutes | Cooking Time: 85 Minutes

Ingredients:

- Crust Layer:
- 1/2 cup flour
- 1/4 cup sugar
- 1/2 teaspoon baking powder
- 1/8 teaspoon salt
- 56-g (1/2 stick) unsalted European style butter, melted
- 1 egg
- 1 teaspoon orange extract
- 2 tablespoons orange zest
- Gooey Butter Layer:
- 226-g cream cheese, softened
- 113-g (1 stick) unsalted European style butter, melted
- 2 eggs
- 2 teaspoons orange extract
- 2 tablespoons orange zest
- 4 cups powdered sugar
- Garnish:
- Powdered sugar
- Orange slices

Directions:

1. Preheat the air fryer to 175°C/350°F.
2. Grease a 18-cm cake pan and line the bottom with parchment paper. Combine the flour, sugar, baking powder and salt in a bowl. Add the melted butter, egg, orange extract and orange zest. Mix well and press this mixture into the bottom of the greased cake pan. Lower the pan into the basket using an aluminum foil sling (fold a piece of aluminum foil into a strip about 5-cm wide by 60-cm long). Fold the ends of the aluminum foil over the top of the dish before returning the basket to the air fryer. Air-fry uncovered for 8 minutes.
3. To make the gooey butter layer, beat the cream cheese, melted butter, eggs, orange extract and orange zest in a large bowl using an electric hand mixer. Add the powdered sugar in stages, beat until smooth with each addition. Pour this mixture on top of the baked crust in the cake pan. Wrap the pan with a piece of greased aluminum foil, tenting the top of the foil to leave a little room for the cake to rise.
4. Air-fry for 60 minutes at 175°C/350°F. Remove the aluminum foil and air-fry for an additional 17 minutes.
5. Let the cake cool inside the pan for at least 10 minutes. Then, run a butter knife around the cake and let the cake cool completely in the pan. When cooled, run the butter knife around the edges of the cake again and invert it onto a plate and then back onto a serving platter. Sprinkle the powdered sugar over the top of the cake and garnish with orange slices.

Variations & Ingredients Tips:

- Use Meyer lemons instead of oranges for a tart lemon flavor.
- Top with candied orange peel or drizzle with an orange glaze.
- Bake in ramekins for individual servings.

Per Serving: Calories: 730; Total Fat: 36g; Saturated Fat: 22g; Cholesterol: 175mg; Sodium: 280mg; Total Carbs: 101g; Dietary Fiber: 1g; Total Sugars: 86g; Protein: 7g

Fried Oreos Recipes

Servings: 12 | Prep Time: 10 Minutes | Cooking Time: 6 Minutes Per Batch

Ingredients:

- oil for misting or nonstick spray
- 1 cup complete pancake and waffle mix
- 1 teaspoon vanilla extract
- ½ cup water, plus 2 tablespoons
- 12 Oreos or other chocolate sandwich cookies
- 1 tablespoon confectioners' sugar

Directions:

1. Spray baking pan with oil or nonstick spray and place in basket.
2. Preheat air fryer to 200°C/390°F.
3. In a medium bowl, mix together the pancake mix, vanilla, and water.
4. Dip 4 cookies in batter and place in baking pan.
5. Cook for 6 minutes, until browned.
6. Repeat steps 4 and 5 for the remaining cookies.
7. Sift sugar over warm cookies.

Variations & Ingredients Tips:

▶ Use different cookie flavors like golden Oreos, snickerdoodles, or chocolate chip.
▶ Mix in cocoa powder, cinnamon, or nutmeg into the batter for extra flavor.
▶ Top with a drizzle of chocolate ganache or a sprinkle of sea salt.

Per Serving: Calories: 140; Total Fat: 6g; Saturated Fat: 1.5g; Sodium: 170mg; Total Carbohydrates: 21g; Dietary Fiber: 0g; Total Sugars: 11g; Protein: 1g

Apple-carrot Cupcakes

Servings: 6 | Prep Time: 10 Minutes | Cooking Time: 25 Minutes

Ingredients:

- 1 cup grated carrot
- 1/3 cup chopped apple
- 1/4 cup raisins
- 2 tbsp maple syrup
- 1/3 cup milk
- 1 cup oat flour
- 1 tsp ground cinnamon
- 1/2 tsp ground ginger
- 1 tsp baking powder
- 1/2 tsp baking soda
- 1/3 cup chopped walnuts

Directions:

1. Preheat air fryer to 175°C/350°F.
2. Combine carrot, apple, raisins, maple syrup, and milk in a bowl.
3. Stir in oat flour, cinnamon, ginger, baking powder, and baking soda until combined.
4. Divide the batter between 6 cupcake molds.
5. Top with chopped walnuts each and press down a little.
6. Bake for 15 minutes until golden brown and a toothpick comes out clean.
7. Let cool completely before serving.

Variations & Ingredients Tips:

▶ Use whole wheat flour instead of oat flour.
▶ Add shredded coconut or dried cranberries.
▶ Top with cream cheese frosting.

Per Serving: Calories: 178; Total Fat: 7g; Saturated Fat: 1g; Sodium: 173mg; Total Carbohydrates: 28g; Dietary Fiber: 3g; Total Sugars: 12g; Protein: 4g

Mini Carrot Cakes

Servings: 6 | Prep Time: 15 Minutes | Cooking Time: 25 Minutes

Ingredients:

- 1 cup grated carrots
- 1/4 cup raw honey
- 1/4 cup olive oil
- 1/2 tsp vanilla extract
- 1/2 tsp lemon zest
- 1 egg
- 1/4 cup applesauce
- 1 1/3 cups flour
- 3/4 tsp baking powder
- 1/2 tsp baking soda
- 1/2 tsp ground cinnamon
- 1/4 tsp ground nutmeg
- 1/8 tsp ground ginger
- 1/8 tsp salt
- 1/4 cup chopped hazelnuts
- 2 tbsp chopped sultanas

Directions:

1. Preheat air fryer to 190°C/380°F.
2. Mix carrots, honey, oil, vanilla, zest, egg and applesauce.
3. In another bowl, sift flour, baking powder, soda, spices and salt.
4. Add dry to wet ingredients and mix just until combined.
5. Fold in hazelnuts and sultanas.
6. Fill greased muffin cups 3/4 full with batter.
7. Place cups in air fryer basket and bake 10-12 mins until a toothpick comes out clean.
8. Serve and enjoy!

Variations & Ingredients Tips:

▶ Use maple syrup or agave instead of honey.
▶ Add raisins, walnuts or shredded coconut.
▶ Top with cream cheese frosting.

Per Serving (2 mini cakes): Calories: 312; Total Fat: 13g; Saturated Fat: 2g; Sodium: 256mg; Total Carbohydrates: 46g; Dietary Fiber: 4g; Total Sugars: 19g; Protein: 5g

Chocolate Cake

Servings: 8 | Prep Time: 10 Minutes | Cooking Time: 20 Minutes

Ingredients:

- 1/2 cup sugar
- 1/4 cup flour, plus 3 tablespoons
- 3 tablespoons cocoa
- 1/2 teaspoon baking powder
- 1/2 teaspoon baking soda
- 1/4 teaspoon salt
- 1 egg
- 2 tablespoons oil
- 1/2 cup milk
- 1/2 teaspoon vanilla extract

Directions:

1. Preheat air fryer to 165°C/330°F.
2. Grease and flour a 15x15cm baking pan.
3. In a bowl, stir together sugar, flours, cocoa, baking powder, soda and salt.
4. Add egg, oil, milk and vanilla. Beat with a whisk until smooth.
5. Pour batter into prepared pan.
6. Bake at 330°F for 20 minutes until toothpick inserted comes out clean.

Variations & Ingredients Tips:

- Add chocolate chips or chopped nuts to the batter.
- Substitute buttermilk for a moister cake.
- Top with chocolate frosting or powdered sugar.

Per Serving: Calories: 149; Total Fat: 4g; Saturated Fat: 1g; Sodium: 158mg; Total Carbohydrates: 26g; Dietary Fiber: 1g; Total Sugars: 14g; Protein: 3g

Berry Streusel Cake

Servings: 6 | Prep Time: 15 Minutes | Cooking Time: 60 Minutes

Ingredients:

- 2 tbsp demerara sugar
- 2 tbsp sunflower oil
- 1/4 cup almond flour
- 1 cup pastry flour
- 1/2 cup brown sugar
- 1 tsp baking powder
- 1 tbsp lemon zest
- 1/4 tsp salt
- 3/4 cup milk
- 2 tbsp olive oil
- 1 tsp vanilla
- 1 cup blueberries
- 1/2 cup powdered sugar
- 1 tbsp lemon juice
- 1/8 tsp salt

Directions:

1. Mix demerara sugar, sunflower oil, and almond flour. Refrigerate.
2. Whisk pastry flour, brown sugar, baking powder, zest, and 1/4 tsp salt.
3. Add milk, olive oil, vanilla and stir until combined. Fold in blueberries.
4. Oil a baking pan and pour in batter.
5. Preheat air fryer to 155°C/310°F.
6. Top batter with chilled almond mixture.
7. Bake for 45 mins until a toothpick inserted comes out clean.
8. Make icing with powdered sugar, lemon juice and 1/8 tsp salt.
9. Let cake cool, slice into 6 pieces and drizzle with icing.

Variations & Ingredients Tips:

- Use raspberries or strawberries instead of blueberries.
- Add sliced almonds or pecans to the streusel topping.
- Substitute buttermilk for regular milk.

Per Serving: Calories: 333; Total Fat: 13g; Saturated Fat: 2g; Sodium: 193mg; Total Carbohydrates: 50g; Dietary Fiber: 3g; Total Sugars: 27g; Protein: 5g

Baked Caramelized Peaches

Servings: 6 | Prep Time: 10 Minutes | Cooking Time: 25 Minutes

Ingredients:

- 3 pitted peaches, halved
- 2 tbsp brown sugar
- 1 cup heavy cream
- 1 tsp vanilla extract
- 1/4 tsp ground cinnamon
- 1 cup fresh blueberries

Directions:

1. Preheat air fryer to 190°C/380°F.
2. Lay the peaches in the frying basket with the cut side up, then top them with brown sugar.
3. Bake for 7-11 minutes, allowing the peaches to brown around the edges.
4. In a mixing bowl, whisk heavy cream, vanilla, and cinnamon until stiff peaks form.
5. Fold the peaches into a plate.
6. Spoon the cream mixture into the peach cups, top with blueberries, and serve.

Variations & Ingredients Tips:

- Use honey or maple syrup instead of brown sugar.
- Add a sprinkle of cinnamon and nutmeg to the cream.
- Top with toasted nuts or granola for crunch.

Per Serving: Calories: 215; Total Fat: 15g; Saturated Fat: 9g; Sodium: 25mg; Total Carbohydrates: 20g; Dietary Fiber: 2g; Total Sugars: 17g; Protein: 2g

Sweet Potato Donut Holes

Servings: 18 | Prep Time: 15 Minutes | Cooking Time: 4 Minutes Per Batch

Ingredients:

- 1 cup flour
- 1/3 cup sugar
- 1/4 teaspoon baking soda
- 1 teaspoon baking powder
- 1/8 teaspoon salt
- 1/2 cup cooked mashed purple sweet potatoes
- 1 egg, beaten
- 2 tablespoons butter, melted
- 1 teaspoon pure vanilla extract
- Oil for misting or cooking spray

Directions:

1. Preheat air fryer to 200°C/390°F.
2. In a large bowl, stir together the flour, sugar, baking soda, baking powder, and salt.
3. In a separate bowl, combine the potatoes, egg, butter, and vanilla and mix well.
4. Add potato mixture to dry ingredients and stir into a soft dough.
5. Shape dough into 3.8cm balls. Mist lightly with oil or cooking spray.
6. Place 9 donut holes in air fryer basket, leaving a little space in between. Cook for 4 minutes, until done in center and lightly browned outside.
7. Repeat step 6 to cook remaining donut holes.

Variations & Ingredients Tips:

- Use other mashed sweet potatoes like white or orange varieties.
- Coat in cinnamon-sugar after cooking.
- Drizzle with a maple glaze.

Per Serving (3 donut holes): Calories: 100; Total Fat: 3g; Saturated Fat: 1.5g; Cholesterol: 25mg; Sodium: 105mg; Total Carbs: 17g; Dietary Fiber: 1g; Total Sugars: 7g; Protein: 2g

Annie's Chocolate Chunk Hazelnut Cookies

Servings: 24 | Prep Time: 20 Minutes | Cooking Time: 12 Minutes

Ingredients:

- 1 cup butter, softened
- 1 cup brown sugar
- 1/2 cup granulated sugar
- 2 eggs, lightly beaten
- 1 1/2 teaspoons vanilla extract
- 1 1/2 cups all-purpose flour
- 1/2 cup rolled oats
- 1 teaspoon baking soda
- 1/2 teaspoon salt
- 2 cups chocolate chunks
- 1/2 cup toasted chopped hazelnuts

Directions:

1. Cream the butter and sugars together until light and fluffy using a stand mixer or electric hand mixer. Add the eggs and vanilla, and beat until well combined.
2. Combine the flour, rolled oats, baking soda and salt in a second bowl. Gradually add the dry ingredients to the wet ingredients with a wooden spoon or spatula.
3. Stir in the chocolate chunks and hazelnuts until distributed throughout the dough.
4. Shape the cookies into small balls about the size of golf balls and place them on a baking sheet. Freeze the cookie balls for at least 30 minutes.
5. Preheat the air fryer to 175°C/350°F.
6. Cut parchment paper to fit and place in the air fryer basket with the frozen cookie balls, leaving room for expansion.

7. Air fry the cookies at 175°C/350°F for 12 minutes, or until desired doneness.
8. Let cool for a few minutes before enjoying.

Variations & Ingredients Tips:

- Use different nut varieties like pecans or walnuts.
- Substitute chocolate chips for the chunks.
- Add shredded coconut to the dough.

Per Serving: Calories: 224; Total Fat: 13g; Saturated Fat: 7g; Sodium: 137mg; Total Carbohydrates: 27g; Dietary Fiber: 2g; Total Sugars: 17g; Protein: 3g

Lemon Iced Donut Balls

Servings: 6 | Prep Time: 10 Minutes | Cooking Time: 25 Minutes

Ingredients:

- 1 can jumbo biscuit dough
- 2 tsp lemon juice
- 1/2 cup icing sugar, sifted

Directions:

1. Preheat air fryer to 180°C/360°F.
2. Divide biscuit dough into 16 equal portions and roll into 3.8-cm balls.
3. Place balls in greased air fryer basket.
4. Air fry for 8 minutes, flipping once halfway.
5. In a bowl, mix icing sugar and lemon juice until smooth.
6. Spread icing over warm donut balls.
7. Let icing set slightly before serving.

Variations & Ingredients Tips:

- Add lemon or orange zest to the icing.
- Roll donut balls in cinnamon-sugar before baking.
- Make a glaze icing by adding milk instead of lemon juice.

Per Serving (3 donut balls): Calories: 211; Total Fat: 5g; Saturated Fat: 2g; Sodium: 282mg; Total Carbohydrates: 39g; Dietary Fiber: 0g; Total Sugars: 14g; Protein: 3g

Recipes Index

A

Air-fried Beignets	90
Air-fried Strawberry Hand Tarts	88
Albóndigas	40
All-in-one Breakfast Toast	11
Almond Topped Trout	54
Almond-crusted Fish	53
Almond-pumpkin Porridge	14
Annie's Chocolate Chunk Hazelnut Cookies	96
Apple-carrot Cupcakes	94
Artichoke-spinach Dip	26
Asian Glazed Meatballs	80
Asian-style Shrimp Toast	22
Asparagus	68
Avocado Egg Rolls	26

B

Bacon Candy	24
Baked Caramelized Peaches	95
Baked Shishito Peppers	74
Banana Bread Cake	91
Banana-blackberry Muffins	13
Banana-lemon Bars	88
Barbecue-style London Broil	45
Beef Short Ribs	43
Beer Battered Onion Rings	27
Berry Streusel Cake	95
Berry-glazed Turkey Breast	33
Black Bean Veggie Burgers	79
Blistered Green Beans	70
Blueberry Applesauce Oat Cake	11
Blueberry Pannenkoek (dutch Pancake)	19
Brown Rice And Goat Cheese Croquettes	75
Brown Sugar Baked Apples	90
Buffalo Wings	19

C

Cajun-seasoned Shrimp	54
Cal-mex Turkey Patties	35
Calf's Liver	47
Carrot-oat Cake Muffins	90
Cauliflower	69
Cauliflower "tater" Tots	25
Cheddar Stuffed Jalapenos	22
Cheddar-bean Flautas	64
Cheeseburger Slider Pockets	20
Cheesy Texas Toast	70
Chicken & Fruit Biryani	33
Chicken Apple Brie Melt	85
Chicken Chunks	35
Chicken Gyros	83
Chicken Pigs In Blankets	35
Chicken Spiedies	83
Chili Cheese Dogs	79
Chili Corn On The Cob	21
Chili Tofu & Quinoa Bowls	60
Chinese Fish Noodle Bowls	52
Chipotle Sunflower Seeds	28
Chive Potato Pierogi	64
Chocolate Cake	95
Classic Salisbury Steak Burgers	39
Coconut Curry Chicken With Coconut Rice	32
Colorful French Toast Sticks	13
Corn & Shrimp Boil	56
Crab Stuffed Salmon Roast	50
Crispy Cauliflower Puffs	72
Crispy Fish Sandwiches	49
Crispy Spiced Chickpeas	24
Crispy Steak Subs	38
Crispy, Cheesy Leeks	69
Crunchy Falafel Balls	86
Crunchy Veal Cutlets	47

D

Daadi Chicken Salad	37
Dark Chocolate Cream Galette	89
Dijon Artichoke Hearts	71
Dijon Thyme Burgers	77

E

Easy Zucchini Lasagna Roll-ups	64
Effortless Mac 'n' Cheese	62
Eggplant Fries	21
Eggplant Parmesan	60
Eggplant Parmesan Subs	87
Enchilada Chicken Dip	23
English Scones	17

F

Feta & Shrimp Pita	49
Fiery Bacon-wrapped Dates	22
Flank Steak With Caramelized Onions	14
Flank Steak With Roasted Peppers And Chimichurri	41
Fried Cauliflower With Parmesan Lemon Dressing	72
Fried Green Tomatoes With Sriracha Mayo	70
Fried Oreos	91
Fried Oreos Recipes	93

G

Garlic And Dill Salmon	53
	100
Garlic Parmesan Bread Ring	15
Garlic-parmesan Popcorn	68
Glazed Carrots	74
Glazed Chicken Thighs	32
Goat Cheese Stuffed Turkey Roulade	31
Grilled Pork & Bell Pepper Salad	42
Ground Beef Calzones	43
Gruyère Asparagus & Chicken Quiche	30

H

Healthy Caprese Salad	68
Homemade Chips Ahoy	92
Honey Pecan Shrimp	51
Hot Cheese Bites	20

I

Inside Out Cheeseburgers	76
Inside-out Cheeseburgers	82
Italian Stuffed Bell Peppers	48
Italian-style Fried Cauliflower	67

J

Jerk Turkey Meatballs	29

L

Lamb Burgers 77

Lamb Meatballs With Quick Tomato Sauce 45

Lemon Herb Whole Cornish Hen 29

Lemon Iced Donut Balls 97

Lemon-blueberry Morning Bread 18

Lemon-dill Salmon Burgers 52

Lemon-roasted Salmon Fillets 56

Lentil Burritos With Cilantro Chutney 59

Lentil Fritters 58

M

Meatloaf With Tangy Tomato Glaze 46

Mediterranean Sea Scallops 57

Mexican Cheeseburgers 81

Mexican Chicken Roll-ups 37

Mexican Twice Air-fried Sweet Potatoes 65

Mini Carrot Cakes 94

Mushroom & Cavolo Nero Egg Muffins 17

Mushroom Lasagna 62

Mushroom-rice Stuffed Bell Peppers 61

Mushroom, Zucchini And Black Bean Burgers 66

Mustard Greens Chips With Curried Sauce 24

N

Nashville Hot Chicken 30

O

Old Bay Lobster Tails 55

Orange Gooey Butter Cake 93

P

Panko-crusted Zucchini Fries 72

Parmesan Fish Bites 50

Party Giant Nachos 67

Perfect Broccoli 71

Perfect Burgers 84

Perfect Pork Chops 42

Pesto Egg & Ham Sandwiches 12

Philly Cheesesteak Sandwiches 76

Pinto Bean Casserole 58

Poblano Bake 33

Popcorn Chicken Tenders With Vegetables 37

Pork Cutlets With Almond-lemon Crust 42

Pork Schnitzel 44

Pork Schnitzel With Dill Sauce 39

Powerful Jackfruit Fritters 66

Provolone Stuffed Meatballs 85

R

Rigatoni With Roasted Onions, Fennel, Spinach And Lemon Pepper Ricotta 61

Roasted Herbed Shiitake Mushrooms 74

Roasted Ratatouille Vegetables 73

Roasted Red Pepper Dip 23

Roasted Tomato And Cheddar Rolls 11

S

Salmon Burgers 80

Salmon Salad With Steamboat Dressing 73

Sausage And Pepper Heros 86

Savory Eggplant Fries 27

Seafood Quinoa Frittata 18

Seasoned Herbed Sourdough Croutons 12

Shrimp Teriyaki 54

Skirt Steak With Horseradish Cream 41

Sloppy Joes 38

Southern Shrimp With Cocktail Sauce 56

Spiced Salmon Croquettes 49

Spicy Chicken And Pepper Jack Cheese Bites 25

Spicy Sesame Tempeh Slaw With Peanut Dressing 63

Spinach-bacon Rollups 18

Sultana & Walnut Stuffed Apples 88

Sushi-style Deviled Eggs 62

Suwon Pork Meatballs 46

Sweet Nutty Chicken Breasts 36

Sweet Plantain Chips 28

Sweet Potato Curly Fries 75

Sweet Potato Donut Holes 96

Sweet Potato–wrapped Shrimp 51

T

Thai-style Pork Sliders	84
Thanksgiving Turkey Sandwiches	78
Thyme Sweet Potato Wedges	69
Tilapia Teriyaki	57
Turkey Burgers	34
Turkey Scotch Eggs	34

V

Vanilla Cupcakes With Chocolate Chips	92
Vegetarian Stuffed Bell Peppers	65
Veggie & Feta Scramble Bowls	15
Vodka Basil Muffins With Strawberries	16

W

Wake-up Veggie & Ham Bake	16
White Bean Veggie Burgers	82
White Wheat Walnut Bread	13
Wiener Schnitzel	44
Windsor's Chicken Salad	36

Y

Yogurt-marinated Chicken Legs	31
Yummy Salmon Burgers With Salsa Rosa	55

Z

Zucchini Tamale Pie	59
Zucchini Walnut Bread	16

Printed in Great Britain
by Amazon